PRAYING THROUGH

# THE 4 0

# PROPHECIES

*with documented fulfillments and
biblical prayer strategies*

# CHRIS REED

WITH CONTRIBUTIONS FROM RICK JOYNER,
MICHAEL FICKESS, MORNINGSTAR JOURNAL NEWS,
AND THE MSU COMPANY OF PROPHETS

*Praying Through the Forty Prophecies*
by Chris Reed
Copyright © 2023

FIRST EDITION (CURRENT AS OF NOVEMBER 2023)

Distributed by MorningStar Publications, Inc.,
A division of MorningStar Fellowship Church
375 Star Light Drive, Fort Mill, SC 29715
www.MorningStarMinistries.org
1-800-542-0278

Printed in the United States of America
Cover design by Esther Eunjoo Jun
Layout design by Michael Fickess

ISBN—978-1-60708-001-5

For a free catalog of MorningStar Resources,
Please call 1-800-542-0278

# Table of Contents

*"Pursue love, and desire spiritual gifts,*
*but especially that you may prophesy."*
—*1 Corinthians 14:1*

# THE COMPANY OF
# PROPHETS
## ⓉMSU

**MORNINGSTAR UNIVERSITY
COMPANY OF PROPHETS CONTRIBUTORS**

LINDSEY DEGRANDPRE
KYLE FARAGHAN
RAMSES GIRGIS
ALISON GRAHAM
OLIVIA HAMM
TARA HEDGES
KAREN HOLBROOK-PRAWER
CALEB LAW
SKYLER LORD
ELISHA MARTINEZ
ELYSE QUEZEL
HANK NUNNALLY
GABRIEL SINCLAIR

MORNINGSTAR UNIVERSITY
SCHOOL OF COMMUNICATIONS CONTRIBUTORS

MAREK ALEXA
ISABELLA LEMOS
CHRIS MARTINEZ
DANIEL ZOU

# MORNINGSTAR JOURNAL NEWS CONTRIBUTORS

DANIEL EMMANUEL
CLIFTON GADBOIS
JENA HARRIS

*"Surely the Lord God does nothing,*
*Unless He reveals His secret to*
*His servants the prophets."*
*—Amos 3:7*

## INTRODUCTORY TEACHING

# The Careful Handling of Contemporary Prophecy

by Michael Fickess

*MorningStar University Director and*
*MorningStar Journal News Director*

There are different ways to pack up and move a home. Think of people on the expressway who have filled their pick-up trucks with dressers, mattresses, and boxes in a tumbled mass, barely held together with twine and bungee cords. This kind of careless packing usually leaves a trail of wreckage scattered across the highway. But those who really value their belongings will properly care for and protect them in the moving process. This is especially true for our most valuable possessions. If you have a priceless family heirloom handed down through the generations, you wouldn't just throw it in the back of a pick-up truck—you would carefully pack it in bubble wrap, label it, and entrust it to a mover with five-star reviews. This is because people who truly value what is entrusted to them handle it with the utmost care. Likewise, when we handle prophecy, it requires a willingness to lay everything aside to really take it seriously and steward it well. Jesus explained,

**"Again, the kingdom of heaven is like a merchant seeking beautiful pearls,**
**"who, when he had found one pearl of great price, went and sold all that he had and bought it" (Matthew 13:45-46).**

When our eyes are first opened to see the kingdom of God advancing around us, then every other pursuit in our lives takes a back seat to a much greater purpose. Compelled by the beauty of God, we become willing to "sell all." Today, God's people are drawn to many different aspects of the kingdom of heaven such as worship, the healing ministry, the house of prayer, or works of missions and charity—and many have "sold all" in order to advance the kingdom through these and many other expressions of the Lord. However, the prophetic ministry remains one of the most compelling, beautiful, and important tools the Lord uses to advance His kingdom on earth.

We have written this book because prophetic words deserve to be taken seriously and handled with care. And you have likely purchased this book because you value the prophetic ministry as much as we do. The many dedicated contributors to this book chose to lay things aside to bring a full and careful analysis of what the Lord has spoken. Now you have chosen to lay other things aside to read this book and commit time to pray about everything the Lord has revealed. Yet even after our work is done, our stewardship of the prophetic ministry does not end simply when a prophetic word is fulfilled or our prayers are answered. Our hope is that after we have properly documented everything the Lord has spoken and done, this prophetic legacy will become a priceless "family heirloom" to inspire future generations, just as the monastic movement, the Moravian legacy, or the records of early healing revivalists have been for us.

# The Praying Mantis and the Watchman Ministry

Over the years, I have noticed an insect that tends to show up as a reminder at strategic times—the praying mantis. The insect's name comes from the Greek word *mantis,* which simply means "prophet." In its resting position, its forelegs appear to be folded in fervent prayer. This unique creature is a reminder of the simple truth that every prophet is also called to pray. This is because authentic prophetic words and fervent prayer are designed to complement one another. Prophetic words are given to us by God in order to guide our prayers so they are more closely aligned with the will of the Father. When Jesus taught the disciples to pray, he modeled a simple and powerful petition to the Father:

**"Your kingdom come, your will be done, on earth as it is in heaven" (Luke 11:2).**

It is powerful to include this invocation in our daily prayers, even if we're not sure what the Lord's will is in a specific situation. In many cases, we ask the Father to "do His will" before we even have a clear picture of what His will is in that specific situation. This is a healthy expression of our trust in God. However, the prophetic ministry is a powerful and mysterious guide for prayer because it reveals the Father's will to us with great precision. Prophetic words allow us to pray with precise strategy and confidence because the prophetic allows us to discern the will of the Father with specific detail. For example, we might be confident in the Lord as our healer based on the clear teaching of scripture, but a prophecy we receive about our healing might provide the details and strategies we need to persevere in prayer when our faith might otherwise falter.

Without prophetic illumination or understanding of Biblical promises, it is common for us to pray with wavering faith because we lack a renewed understanding of the Father's desire for us.

11

Prophetic promises often remind us of the eternal promises of scripture and the Father's unwavering character: as a result, our faith is renewed and regenerated so we can pray with confidence again. In other words, the prophetic is designed to propel us into a powerful, exciting, and faith-charged prayer life.

## "Warring with the Prophecies"

I have seen thousands of lives deeply impacted by prophetic ministry over the last three decades. Cancers have been healed and arthritic joints mended because accurate prophetic ministry inspired faith and confidence in the promises and character of God. In most cases, the prophetic ministry is profoundly inspirational because it directs our attention back to the Lord's unchanging promises and eternal character. In its purest form, prophetic ministry reveals the nearness of God, the reality of God, and the love of God. Yet not all prophecy is initially interpreted as encouraging: the Lord also gives words of warning or correction to people that can bear just as much fruit as an encouraging word when the truth is "spoken in love" (Ephesians 4:15).

With interpersonal prophecy, the Lord often speaks to people just as he spoke to the seven churches of Asia Minor in the book of Revelation. He offers affirmation and profound promises for the future in order to encourage and build up others (1 Corinthians 14:3). Sometimes, He even reveals details from the past to assure them He has been with them all along and deeply loves them. He also gives correction, rebuke, and guidance in areas where they have stepped off the path of life. Watchman words for America, Israel, and the nations of the earth also cover this full spectrum: it is not enough to hear words that simply "tickle our ears" (2 Timothy 4:3). In fact, if we really care about the nations, we will *want* to hear the unvarnished truth so that we can take the steps needed to correct our course.

If we study American revival history, we will find the first and second Great Awakenings were not preceded by a flurry of stimulating, ear-tickling encouragement—but rather by bold and confrontational preaching that exposed wickedness, warned of impending judgment, and called the nation to heart-rending repentance. This pattern is so well-established that even the most godless historians have referred to it as the "American Jeremiad" and noted the centrality of words of warning throughout our history. The awakenings prompted by these words of warning did not merely lead to a spiritual revival—they had a wide impact on all of society, inspiring the American Revolution as well as the end of slavery in the United States.

Accurate watchman words equip us for more effective spiritual warfare. For example, the proper way to respond to accurate interpersonal prophetic ministry is to use it as a springboard for prayer. This is why Paul wrote to Timothy:

**"Timothy, my son, here are my instructions for you, based on the prophetic words spoken about you earlier. May they help you fight well in the Lord's battles" (1 Timothy 1:18 NLT).**

When we are in the midst of difficult personal battles, we need to war with the words we have been given: the same principle applies to watchman words about the nations. The Father entrusts the kind of highly accurate words contained in this book so we can use them to discern the Lord's plans and pray in concert with heaven's counsel. Of course, this kind of lofty goal seems harder to reach when many of these words could be characterized as "negative." After all, what are we supposed to pray when there are accurate words unfolding about war, terrorism, government corruption, and food shortages? The many contributors to this book have pored over these prophecies and connected them to current events and scripture in order to present some clear and Biblical prayer strategies. Hopefully, this will help to contextualize each word and build faith for what God wants to do. However, in order to really understand the larger context for what is unfolding, we need to see the "macro-view"— or the larger picture of the Lord's plans for the end times.

## The Two-Sided Coin of the End-Times

It was the best of times, it was the worst of times, it was the age of wisdom, it was the age of foolishness, it was the epoch of belief, it was the epoch of incredulity, it was the season of Light, it was the season of Darkness, it was the spring of hope, it was the winter of despair, we had everything before us, we had nothing before us, we were all going direct to Heaven, we were all going direct the other way…

Like Dickens' description above which opens *The Tale of Two Cities*, a careful study of scripture reveals that the end of the age is like a two-sided coin. On one side, we see in scripture the clear promises of a massive global harvest of souls, an outpouring of the Spirit greater than the book of Acts, entire nations being discipled, and the kingdom of heaven advancing on earth in ways that defy what we could even begin to imagine. This is the side of the coin that I call "HARVEST AND GLORY." On the other side, we see promises of natural disaster, economic collapse, war, deception, wickedness, and pestilence that may **"cause [our] hearts to fail within [us]" (Luke 21:26).** This is the side of the coin that I call "SHAKING AND JUDGMENT."

It seems many in the Body of Christ have an incomplete view of what to expect in the end times because they are focused exclusively on one side of the coin and generally fall into camps. One camp boldly announces that we are already in the "Kingdom Age" and that things will only be "tulips and buttercups" from here until eternity. The other camp is focused on dire warning words and has little hope for any significant revival or restoration to come before Christ returns. As a result of these excesses, most believers are left unprepared for what is coming. One camp is

14

unprepared for the coming harvest and glory and the other camp is unprepared for the imminent shaking and judgment.

A complete view of the end times considers the full weight of scripture and seeks to prepare for everything the Lord has in store. However, we are meant to understand even more than this: the reality is that the "shaking and judgment" to come will be used by God to wake up the Body of Christ and initiate much of the "harvest and greater glory" that has been promised. In other words, the two sides of the coin work together because in most cases, the judgments of the Lord are redemptive in nature. He shakes us up in order to wake us up. For example, many of the 40 prophecies in this volume involve the exposure of government corruption. At first glance, these appear to be devastating warnings about the broken state of the U.S. Government. However, a more redemptive view can discern that the exposure and removal of corruption could lead to a season of unprecedented governmental reform—just as someone who is caught in sin can be brought to repentance and restoration. When we can see both sides of the coin and how they work together like this, then it becomes easier to develop clear strategy for intercession.

One of the best ways to understand the shaking God is allowing is to read Christ's message to Laodicea, which is a message to much of the Body of Christ today. The Laodicean church was "lukewarm...wretched, poor, blind, and naked" and yet they considered themselves to be rich and "in need of nothing" (Rev. 3:15-17). Likewise, Western culture is primarily materialistic. Instead of putting our trust in God, we have put our trust in our wealth, our government institutions, and a level of comfort that goes far beyond any other civilization in history. And so, it is out of His deep love for us that the Lord will allow the idols we have trusted in to be shaken so that we can return to Him.

# Categorizing and Praying Through Warning Words

Complex prophecies require complex analysis. Since this book is primarily about understanding and praying through warning words, it is important to understand the difference between the different kinds of prophetic warning we may encounter, which include (1) conditional prophecy, (2) redemptive judgment, (2) warnings of enemy activity, (4) sign prophecies, and (5) warnings of coming wrath.

## 1. Conditional Prophecy

Conditional prophecy involves warnings or promises that depend upon the choices we make. The clearest set of conditional prophecies in scripture is in Deuteronomy 28, which lists a set of remarkable blessings for Israel that they would receive *only if* they hear and obey God's voice. It also lists a set of devastating judgments for Israel that they would receive *only if* they forsake God and worship idols. Conditional prophecies hinge upon the *if* because our choice to either continue in wickedness or repent has dramatic consequences, both at the individual and the national level.

There are many clear examples of conditional prophetic warnings in scripture. For example, God said that He would have spared Sodom from destruction *only if* there were "ten righteous" in the city (Genesis 18). In contrast, Nineveh faced the same fate as Sodom because it was implied that they would escape destruction *only if* they chose to repent. Many people forget that the prophecy for Nineveh did eventually come true precisely as Jonah prophesied, but the prophecy was delayed by nearly 200 years because the people repented. God waited two centuries to fulfill his word because its fulfillment had an implied condition.

16

The pattern of conditional prophecy also continues throughout the New Testament. In his warnings of Jerusalem's destruction, Jesus urged believers to **"pray that your flight will not be in winter or on the sabbath"** because our prayers are so powerful that they can actually impact God's timeline of events (Matthew 24:20). Even the book of Revelation, which most people view as set in stone, lists prophetic words for the seven churches which include promises believers will receive *only if* they repent and become overcomers of the evil in our time (see Revelation, chapters 2-3).

When we pray about conditional prophecies, the best strategy is to pray specifically that the Lord will work in hearts and minds to stir them to turn from wickedness, repent, and return to Him. But before we ask the Lord to hold back his judgment—or keep a prophetic warning from coming to pass—we must consider whether the event he warned about will actually be used as a tool to turn hearts and minds that might otherwise remain complacent. In other words, we must remain mindful of how God also uses times of difficulty to accomplish His greater purpose.

## 2. Redemptive Judgment

Redemptive judgment manifests the Father's love because it is designed to help us correct our course when we are headed for self-destruction. In redemptive judgment, the Lord allows trials and difficulty to come upon a nation in order to compel us to reconsider our ways and return to Him. In most cases, redemptive judgment simply involves us seeing the *national consequences* of the *national choices* we have made. This is why the scriptures tell us, **"For the Lord disciplines *and* corrects those whom He loves" (Hebrews 12:6 AMP).**

Just as proper discipline is an act of love for our children that allows them to experience the natural consequences of their actions, redemptive judgment is a form of correction from the Lord that is meant to save us from destruction. Redemptive judgment helps us wake up, assess the results of the poor choices we have made, and make dramatic course corrections—leading to national reform or sustained and widespread spiritual awakening. For example, if God is giving warnings about the exposure of government corruption (a frequent theme in this book), it is because he wants us to deal with the wickedness at work and set about reforming the system through prayer and civic action. Likewise, the prophetic warnings about terrorism coming across the border can be used to call us to a place of demanding a return to Biblical principles in how we steward national boundaries and immigration. Even with prophetic warnings about our food supply, we must consider the extent to which we have sacrificed Biblical stewardship of the earth for cheap technological shortcuts that defile the land and poison the water. In all these things, God will allow us to see the consequences of self-destructive choices so that our nation may have the chance to repent and make more righteous choices in the future.

In praying through redemptive judgments that are designed to help a nation correct course, it is generally not our goal to ask God to restrain His hand. Rather, it is our goal to see a clear vision of the creative work He wants to do *through* everything He is allowing. In this sense, we might imagine redemptive judgment as a plow turning the soil of a weed-infested and broken land. Redemptive judgment allows an unfruitful nation to become fruitful again because it gives us a new start in the same way that a backyard garden can be replanted when Spring arrives again.

## 3. Warnings of Enemy Activity

Jesus made it clear that the devil came only to **"kill, steal, and destroy" (John 10:10)**. Just as a good shepherd will call his sheep to return to him at nightfall or when a predator is near, the Lord will warn us and call us to draw near to Him when danger is approaching. We are sometimes unable to understand the true nature of every warning we have been given, but returning to the Lord and pursuing intimacy with Him is always our best defense.

As prophetic watchmen, it is our job to amplify warnings about enemy activity that come from the Lord. The Biblical model included both watchmen on the wall and gatekeepers. In ancient times, the watchman on the wall could see the enemy coming from afar and warn the gatekeepers to shut the city gates so the enemy could not gain access to "kill, steal, or destroy" its inhabitants. Likewise, warnings of enemy activity can in many cases lead to a complete prevention of the harm the enemy intended but *only if* the gatekeepers heed the call and do their job.

Sometimes the gates are barred to the enemy by sustained and unified intercession. And intercessory prayer remains our greatest weapon through all that will unfold in the end times. However, there are other times when we need to deliver warnings to gatekeepers in other sectors. For example, the warnings of terrorism in this book are clear warnings of enemy activity, for terrorism is one of the ultimate expressions of the demonic impulse to "kill, steal, and destroy." It is good to join in sustained intercession about this dire warning. However, we also need to deliver this warning to gatekeepers at our borders, law enforcement in our cities, and ordinary citizens so that practical precautions can also be set in place to prevent acts of terror.

## 4. Sign Prophecies

Scripture tells us that prophecy is a "sign" for believers (1 Corinthians 14:22 ESV). In order to understand prophecy as a sign, we first have to understand the purpose of a sign. Whether we are talking about stoplights, billboards, or street names, signage is usually designed to bring something important to our attention. Signs show us the way, redirect us, prevent disaster, and safely deliver us to our destination. Signs are generally bright, colorful, and bold so that they will arrest our attention. Likewise, sign prophecies get our attention because they are unusual or dramatic. For example, Chris' prophecy of an airplane being lost and then found again is one of the most unusual prophecies I have ever heard. But the question is, what are "signs" like this prophecy pointing us to?

The first and most important purpose of sign prophecies is to serve as a sign that God is real, He is with us, and He knows everything. In a materialistic world that questions the reality of spiritual things, accurate prophecy serves as a sign to believers and unbelievers alike that God is still real and with us. This is why scripture tells us a common response to prophecy should be for an unbeliever to **"fall down on his face, worship God and report that God is truly among you" (1 Corinthians 14: 25).** While conditional prophecies call for action, redemptive judgments call for course correction, and warning prophecies call for spiritual warfare, sign prophecies often inspire worship.

Sign prophecies can also serve as warnings or promises with an exclamation point. For example, the missing plane was prophesied to be an intelligence asset. It is remarkable that this word was fulfilled with precision, but it is also a sign that highlights our need to stop being careless with our national intelligence assets. In this way, sign prophecies also serve to highlight and reinforce what the Lord wants us to understand.

## 5. Warnings of Coming Wrath

It is often difficult for people to reconcile the truth of a loving and redemptive God with the concept of God's wrath. The simple definition of wrath is *extreme anger*. And when God gets extremely angry, the manifestation of that wrath is total destruction. Here, we must understand that the wrath of God is actually an expression of His love. To understand this more fully, let us consider what we believe about eternity: When Christ returns to restore all things, we believe He will restore heaven and earth, give us our glorified bodies, and "wipe every tear from our eyes" as the curse of sin and death is removed from all of creation (see Revelation 21). Even the painful memories of this life will be stripped of all grief and trauma. But such a beautiful restoration would not be possible if He allowed the wicked to remain in the world. The removal of wickedness through His wrath is essential to the beautiful restoration that will follow.

If arsonists and violent thieves invaded my home while I was away, I could not restore my home or comfort my family until I first dealt with the intruders. In fact, I would zealously do whatever is necessary to deal with the intruders because of the deep love I have for my family and my home. I would only be able to restore the burned places in my home or bandage the wounds left by violence after I had removed the intruders from the picture entirely. In the same way, even God's wrath has a redemptive purpose. He will remove wickedness from the earth because His full vision of restoration can only be achieved when evil is fully exposed and removed.

Generally, God's wrath is reserved for the final judgment. Until then, we always have the hope of Nineveh—that even in the face of devastating warnings of destruction, repentance can save our nation. However, there are instances of God's wrath in this life as well—but usually only after a time of repentance has been granted. For example, even the ISIS jihadists that raped and murdered thousands of Christians and Zoroastrians in northern Iraq were given two years to repent. But when that time was up, they faced the wrath of God: the ISIS fighters were slaughtered and piled into mass graves, experiencing the same violence they showed towards others in a destructive judgment that God most certainly allowed. The reason that warnings of wrath should be considered today is because we have been given *a lot* of time to repent and the stakes are much higher now than they have ever been. This is why we take the prophecies in this book so seriously.

## A Collaborative Effort

I have often heard Rick Joyner preach that effective stewardship of the prophetic must include three kinds of people —**"prophets, wise men, and scribes"** (see Matthew 23:34). This is why our effort to steward Chris' forty prophecies with excellence involved convening a group of these kinds of people. Since I am in the unique position of leading both MSJN and MSU, it seemed natural to bring these two MorningStar ministry departments together in a collaborative project that could have a wide impact on the Body of Christ and on the nation.

Our *MorningStar Journal News (MSJN)* team has now been carefully researching and scribing for years as they connect the dots between prophecy, current events, and a biblical worldview in our weekly shows and on our news aggregation website. They have carefully documented how each prophetic word was fulfilled and compiled a long list of credible sources.

Our *MorningStar University Company of Prophets* is a new academic major that we introduced this year. However, the idea of prophets convening together to carefully weigh prophetic words and pray through them is not a new concept. In our weekly sessions, we have spent time building unity, sharing what the Lord is saying, and weighing each prophetic word. The Company of Prophets students have been immensely helpful in

22

supplementing each prophetic word with biblical perspective and strategic prayer points. Our *MorningStar University School of Communications* students have also worked alongside the MSJN team to refine and edit this book.

## The Format of this Book

The format of this book reflects the values that MorningStar holds as a prophetic ministry. One of the best ways for us to train and equip the Body of Christ for prophetic ministry is by stewarding the words we have been given with excellence. This is why the features included in our presentation of each of the forty prophecies include rigorous research and analysis to document what the Lord has fulfilled, an honest assessment of what has not yet come to pass, a strong biblical foundation, and guidance for intercession. While we tried to follow a predictable pattern throughout the 40 Prophecies section, there were several cases where we adjusted the kind of information we shared to reflect what the Holy Spirit was leading us to share.

### a. Gauging the Fulfillment of Prophecy

Some prophecies are really simple and it is easy to tell if they were fulfilled or not. Other prophecies are more complex and may include a series of events that happen over a longer period of time. For this reason, we have used a "fulfillment gauge" to indicate whether a prophecy is not yet fulfilled, is already fulfilled with precision, or is still in the process of being fulfilled. In many cases, there are precise details that *have* been fulfilled, while other details have not yet come to pass. The fulfillment gauge allows us to show the reader where each word falls on this spectrum of fulfillment. Here, it may be important to note that Chris did not share these words as prophecies that would be exclusively fulfilled in 2023—he shared them as words for "2023 *and beyond.*" While some words have already been precisely fulfilled, this book is likely to be a relevant guide to what will still be unfolding for years to come.

## b. Documenting Complete and Partial Fulfillments

Both complete and partial fulfillments are documented in this book on the same page where each prophecy appears. We used the MLA citation format so that the reader can see a shortened form of our source immediately after each documented fulfillment in parenthesis or visit the bibliography to read our sources for themselves. Our goal was to build faith by demonstrating the accuracy and credibility of real prophetic ministry.

## c. Key Scriptures and Biblical Principles

Whether we are processing prophetic insight or praying with fervor, the best compass remains the eternal truth of the scriptures. Our faith and confidence grow when we immerse ourselves in the truth of the Word, which is why we are told, **"faith *comes* by hearing, and hearing by the word of God" (Romans 10:17).** We want the reader to have every opportunity to see their faith grow—faith in what God can do through the prophetic ministry, but also faith for what God can do in Israel, America, and the nations when we respond to prophetic warnings with sustained prayer.

## d. Prayer Strategies and Model Prayers

Instead of letting the reader puzzle over each prophecy before conceiving of a way to respond to it, we wanted to offer guidance for every reader to launch right into prayer by giving either clear strategies for prayers or model prayers to respond to each prophecy. We are confident that when you begin to pray with some of the strategies we have shared, the Spirit will also inspire you with many more prayers that we perhaps did not see. While some may use this as a textbook or a small-group study, it may also serve as a daily devotional for those who want to build their capacity for watchman prophecy and prayer.

# The Context for the Forty Prophecies

### by Chris Reed
*President, MorningStar Ministries*

The context in which the Lord speaks is important for us to understand. That's why I want to show you the backstory for the forty prophecies I shared at our *MorningStar Vision Conference* on December 29, 2022. Since you've picked up this book, you're probably aware that much of what was shared that night has already started to come to pass. The accuracy of what the Lord revealed to me has generated a lot of interest and excitement. But I wanted to show you the process that led to this series of revelations because I want to teach you how the prophetic process works in terms of receiving revelation, scribing it, releasing it at the right time, and tracking its fulfillment.

## My Process for Scribing Revelation

"Write the vision and make *it* plain on tablets, that he may run who reads it.

"For the vision *is* yet for an appointed time; but at the end it will speak, and it will not lie. Though it tarries, wait for it; because it will surely come, it will not tarry."
—Habakkuk 2:2-3

Habakkuk wasn't the first prophet to write down the revelation that God gave him. The process of scribing revelation has always been central to the prophetic ministry. You may have a journal of your own where you write down what the Lord is saying or jot down prophetic dreams when you first wake up. Others may type the revelations they get on a computer, while artists have the ability to draw and paint the revelation. In my case, I tend to scribe the revelation I receive on my cell phone in my notes section. One of the benefits of this process for me is that every prophetic note I make on my phone results in a clear and verifiable time stamp from when each note was first written and saved.

The time-stamped and documented screenshots of these prophecies are important to me because I place a high value on integrity, credibility, and prophetic accountability. I have already shared these screenshots on our *Prophetic Perspectives* and *MSJN Weekly Report* shows on several occasions [available to watch now on www.MorningStarTV.com] as well as on other shows. My goal in being really open about my process and how all of this revelation is documented is to build greater faith to move in the prophetic in every person who sees one of these shows—or anyone who reads this book. You can turn to Appendix 3 of this book to view some samples of my screenshot documentation process if you'd like to look into this more deeply. I want to be rigorous in my approach because I want you to know that God is still speaking today and He is inviting you today to hear from

Him in new ways. When we properly scribe out what we are getting from the Lord, it brings our stewardship of the prophetic to the next level of excellence so that God can trust us with more.

## The Time Frame for When I Received Revelation for the 40 Prophecies

I believe the Lord is calling us to take the prophetic ministry to a higher level. And so, an intensive time of preparation for the 40 Prophecies message really began for me back in October of 2022, when I was fasting, praying, and asking God to begin to show me what was coming in the new year (2023). I prepared for three months to share this set of revelations because I take what the Lord shows me very seriously—especially when the revelations warn of very serious events about to unfold. However, many of these revelations happened much earlier—long before this three-month season of inquiring of the Lord began.

Many of the revelations that I shared in the 40 Prophecies message were given to me three or four years prior to that—in 2018, 2019, and 2020. This was long before I moved to MorningStar in July of 2021 or shared them at the Vision Conference in December of 2022. I shared some of these revelations in previous years at the church in Indiana where I pastored for 12 years. The notes on my phone document this longer time frame in which the Lord gave me this set of revelations. I scribed out everything he told me in those years because I knew it was important—but now that we are in the time of fulfillment, that documentation is valuable for lending credibility to the words the Lord has entrusted to me and for building faith in those who see these things come to pass.

## Praying Through the 40 Prophecies

**"So the Lord relented from the harm which He said He would do to His people."—Exodus 32:14**

Some prophecies are set in stone because the Lord has made up his mind, just as he did many times in scripture when he gave unconditional promises or heavy judgments. But I'm also hopeful because there are many times prayer or human responsiveness can change the outcome of a warning the Lord has given or lessen the effects of it.

For instance, in the New Testament, after the cross, we see Agabus prophesying about a worldwide famine:

"**And in these days prophets came from Jerusalem to Antioch.**

"**Then one of them, named Agabus, stood up and showed by the Spirit that there was going to be a great famine throughout all the world, which also happened in the days of Claudius Caesar.**

"**Then the disciples, each according to his ability, determined to send relief to the brethren dwelling in Judea.**

"**This they also did, and sent it to the elders by the hands of Barnabas and Saul."—Acts 11:27-30**

When he prophesied this international word, the church responded with disaster relief and helped those whom they could. They took action to *lessen the negative effects* of what was prophesied. In another case, Agabus gave a personal prophecy:

**And as we stayed many days, a certain prophet named Agabus came down from Judea.**

**When he had come to us, he took Paul's belt, bound his *own* hands and feet, and said, "Thus says the Holy Spirit, 'So shall the Jews at Jerusalem bind the man who owns this belt, and deliver *him* into the hands of the Gentiles.'"**

**Now when we heard these things, both we and those from that place pleaded with him not to go up to Jerusalem. Then Paul answered, "What do you mean by weeping and breaking**

my heart? For I am ready not only to be bound, but also to die at Jerusalem for the name of the Lord Jesus."

So when he would not be persuaded, we ceased, saying, "The will of the Lord be done."—Acts 21:10-14

Agabus told Paul that if he went to Jerusalem, he would be arrested. Well, Paul went anyway because he believed God told him to go there and he chose to be obedient to the Lord's leading no matter what. So, in one case, the prophetic warning could be lessened and in the other case, there was nothing that could be done. Some things can be changed through prayer and some things can't. Hopefully, this book will help us mobilize in prayer so that the Lord's plans will be advanced and the enemy's plans will be thwarted.

## The Time Frame for the
## 40 Prophecies' Fulfillment

When I first shared these revelations at the Vision Conference, I made it clear that these words were for "2023 and beyond." At that time, I explained to people that I wasn't in a hurry and I wouldn't be disappointed "if these words didn't all happen by February," because I knew it was more likely that these words would unfold over a longer period of time. So I was surprised when only a few days after the conference, the "Biden Boxes" of classified documents were found exactly as I had just prophesied. Since then, many of the prophecies have been rapidly fulfilled or are in the process of being fulfilled. However, others have not yet come to pass.

We're putting out this book now for two reasons: First, the prophecies that have already been fulfilled have really impacted the Body of Christ, renewed interest in the prophetic ministry, and even caught the attention of some important world leaders. We want to be good stewards of what the Lord entrusts to us and get the meat out "in due season"—especially at a time when there is so much turmoil and uncertainty (Matthew 24:45). We also want to have an impact on the world, not just on the Body of Christ. There's no question that the world is hungry for the supernatural, so we believe that documented and accurately fulfilled prophecy can have a really big impact across the board.

The second reason we are releasing this book is that many of the most intense and world-shaking events that were prophesied in these pages have not yet come to pass. These are events such as food shortages, terrorist attacks, and global conflicts that demand a coordinated response from the Body of Christ. Our hope is that by presenting them in this way, the Lord will be glorified and many thousands will be inspired to intercede for America, Israel, and the nations in these tumultuous times.

## Faith, Hope, and Love

Sometimes, people get so caught up with what ministries are releasing on social media or the latest trends that they forget the simple and enduring parts of our faith in Christ. No matter what happens, God wants you to know He loves you, He has a plan for you, and you are called to become an on-fire disciple-making believer who will lead many others to the Lord and teach them how to follow Him, even in times of difficulty.

Some of the people reading this will start house churches, even in the middle of all that will unfold—maybe even in a room that is right now a "man cave." Others will move in the word of knowledge or healing whenever they are out in public to reach out and share the Gospel of Jesus Christ with folks at Wal-Mart, neighbors, and co-workers. As all of these things unfold, we are not victims and we're not powerless because, **"Jesus Christ is the same: yesterday, today, and forever" (Hebrews 13:8).** He won't leave you when times get tough, His promises won't expire, and His blood will never lose its power! These are indeed exciting times to live in and all of our staff here at MorningStar Ministries are grateful that we get to navigate them *with you.*

# The Forty Prophecies

*Including Documented Fulfillments,*
*Biblical Principles, and Prayer Strategies*

*"But there is a God in heaven*
*who reveals mysteries"*
*—Daniel 2:28*

**1**

> "I saw an exposure of Chinese money and bribery. The beginnings of this will include a major exposure which will begin the downfall of the Biden administration."

## FULFILLMENT: Partly Fulfilled

## What has already happened to fulfill this word?

- Classified documents, tax documents, and bank records have revealed that the Biden family received between 50-100 million dollars in payments from Chinese operatives in exchange for political influence (Altus, 2023).
- E-mails from the Hunter Biden laptop reveal that President Biden funneled money through other family members, most notably Hunter, in order to financially enrich himself (United States House Committee on Oversight and Accountability).
- In summary, we have seen the first part of this word fulfilled: it is clear that a pattern of Chinese bribery has been exposed.

## What has not yet happened?

While corruption has already been exposed, it has not yet led to the full "downfall of the Biden administration," which would presumably happen with either an impeachment in Congress or with the election of a different president in 2024.

## Biblical Principles Related to this Word

- In the book of Esther, Haman was an influential man who resorted to bribery in order to accomplish his political goals. Yet this would lead to his very own fall. In the same way, Biden's bribery will be exposed to the public, and the downfall of his administration will begin.
- At the personal level, God exposes and reveals corruption in individuals through the Holy Spirit's conviction so that they can respond with heartfelt repentance (John 16:8).
- At the governmental level, God exposes and reveals corruption so that reformation can come through legitimate means such as elections, congressional action, or criminal prosecution. We have the obligation to respond with prayer and civic action when we see corruption in our leaders (Romans 13).

## Key Scriptures to Read and Pray Through

"For nothing is secret that will not be revealed, nor anything hidden that will not be known and come to light."—Luke 8:17

"And have no fellowship with the unfruitful works of darkness, but rather expose them."—Ephesians 5:11

"The king gives stability to the land by justice, but the man who takes bribes overthrows it."—Proverbs 29:4

## Prayer Strategies

- Pray that "hidden works of darkness," including corruption, will continue to come to light for the greater purpose of future government reformation.
- Take time for introspection and ask the Lord to search your heart and reveal any corruption that you need to repent of.

**2**

"The Hunter Biden laptop case, which was suppressed
before the 2020 election, is about to be opened.
This issue will become a centerfold in the news and will
tremendously hurt his father's credibility and past claims.
Last year, the Lord showed me this would hurt his father to
the point to where he will lose power and be out of office
before the 2024 election."

## FULFILLMENT: Mostly Fulfilled

## What has already happened to fulfill this word?

- In October 2020, the FBI received a flash drive containing emails and text messages from Tony Bobulinski, a business partner of Hunter Biden. This evidence confirmed the authenticity of the contents on Hunter's laptop, contradicting earlier claims of "disinformation."
- The FBI documented this verification in a report. The report also revealed that Joe Biden had personal discussions with Bobulinski regarding his son's lucrative Chinese joint venture. Furthermore, it indicated Joe Biden was set to receive a share of the profits, challenging previous denials (Sperry, 2023).
- The Hunter Biden laptop story has resurfaced in the media this year. This has exposed inconsistencies in Joe Biden's previous statements, significantly undermining his credibility.

## What has not yet happened?

While Hunter Biden's Laptop case has made headlines this year and posed challenges for the president, we are yet to witness Joe Biden "out of office before the 2024 election."

## Biblical Principles Related to this Word

- Eli was a man of significant authority, yet he had disobedient sons whom he failed to discipline. He would go on to lose the priesthood forever as a result of this. In the same way, it will be the shameful acts of Hunter Biden that will cost his father his seat of authority *(See 1 Samuel 2:12-36 to read the story in full).*
- While Romans 13 exhorts us to intercede for our national leaders, including "kings and all those in authority," there are also many biblical and historical precedents for the Lord deposing or removing unrighteous leaders by His sovereignty for the greater benefit of His people and the nations in which they dwell.

## Key Passage to Read and Pray Through

¹ Why do the nations rage, and the people plot a vain thing?
² The kings of the earth set themselves, and the rulers take counsel together, against the Lord and against His Anointed, *saying,*
³ "Let us break their bonds in pieces and cast away their cords from us."
⁴ He who sits in the heavens shall laugh; the Lord shall hold them in derision.
⁵ Then He shall speak to them in His wrath, and distress them in His deep displeasure:
⁶ "Yet I have set My King on my holy hill of Zion." (Psalm 2:1-6)

## Model Prayer

"Father, we know that you are the One who brings down one king and sets up another. We are grateful that you reign supreme and govern the affairs of men. We ask that you bring about what you have spoken—depose unrighteous leaders of our nation and raise up champions of righteousness who can lead us into a time of national restoration, so that the inhabitants of our nation might know that you are God. In Jesus name, Amen."

## 3

"President Joe Biden's health will continue to fail.
I do not wish him harm. I pray for him. I pray for God to
remove him, but I also pray for him and his salvation
and for him to become a Saul of Tarsus figure."

"He will lose power, and it will be convenient for
the Democrats to not have him leading the 2024 ticket.
He will attempt to redeem his failed presidency by making
a woman president for the first time.
I have seen Kamala Harris at the helm, but only for a
short time—weeks or months."

## FULFILLMENT: Partly Fulfilled

## What has already happened to fulfill this word?

- As it stands now, President Biden will not finish. Prominent Democrats have raised questions regarding Joe Biden's age and expressed concerns about his health. Some within the party withhold their support for Biden's 2024 candidacy for this reason (Olorunnipa, 2023).
- A poll has revealed that 68% of voters expressed worries, including 55% with "major" concerns about Joe Biden's health. Notably, concerns about Biden's ability to hold office have grown among Democrats, from 21% in 2020 to 43% now (Todd, 2023).

### What has not yet happened?

While there have been ongoing concerns about Joe Biden's health within the Democratic party, we have yet to see Democrats dismissing him as their 2024 presidential candidate officially, paving the way for Kamala Harris to become the first woman to be president of the U.S.

## Biblical Principles Related to this Word

- While we do not delight in the illness or suffering of anyone, sometimes the Lord will allow these things in order to "raise up" or "tear down" leaders according to His sovereign will (Jeremiah 1:10).
- There is biblical precedent for the Lord afflicting a leader in order to accomplish his greater purpose. For example, the Lord struck King Nebuchadnezzar with madness in order to humble him because of his godlessness and pride as the king of ancient Babylon (Daniel 4). Likewise, it was the Lord Jesus Christ himself who struck Paul with blindness in order to turn his heart from persecuting Christians to being a great apostle (Acts 9). In a similar manner to these examples, the Lord may use President Biden's health issues or mental decline to accomplish his greater purposes—which includes the disqualification of Biden from running for reelection or his personal salvation.
- In Daniel chapter 5, the Lord sent a hand to write on the wall to write an ominous message for the king that Daniel interpreted as, **"You have been weighed in the balances, and found wanting…" (Daniel 5:27).** The remainder of this prophecy warned of the invasion of the Medes and Persians, which happened that very night. Likewise, this prophecy from Chris indicates the Lord's hand will remove Biden from power.

## Key Scriptures to Read and Pray Through

**"King Nebuchadnezzar, to you it is spoken: the kingdom has departed from you! And they shall drive you from men, and your dwelling *shall be* with the beasts of the field. They shall make you eat grass like oxen; and seven times shall pass over you, until you know that the Most High rules in the kingdom of men, and gives it to whomever He chooses."**
**—Daniel 4:31b-32**

## 4

"Unfortunately, we will see a continued rise in inflation and a nosedive in residential and commercial real estate values. There will be a significant housing mortgage crisis, but not as bad as 2008. Precious metals and land will become better, safer investments."

## FULFILLMENT: Partly Fulfilled

## What has already happened to fulfill this word?

- Inflation has remained persistently high despite the Federal Reserve's interest rate hikes. As of late 2023, the annual inflation rate was estimated at around 3.7% from the previous year—higher than the optimal rate of 2% (Rugaber, 2023).
- Mortgage demand has hit a 28-year low, driven by a surge in long-term mortgage rates. According to the Mortgage Bankers Association, the average rate for a 30-year home loan reached 7.53%, the highest since the year 2000. The rising rates are making home ownership less affordable and are affecting the overall housing market, causing sales to decline significantly (Thaler, 2023).

## What has not yet happened?

While housing prices continue at a reasonable level, there is a noticeable dip in mortgage demand and, consequently, in the real estate market. In the foreseeable future, this could bring a decline in housing prices, driven by the surge in mortgage rates resulting from higher interest rates.

## Biblical Principles Related to this Word

- The Lord gave Joseph prophetic insight concerning an economic crisis during ancient times and he was able to receive and implement a strategy that sustained the masses. Likewise, God can raise up "Josephs" today who hear from heaven and develop plans to sustain others when times are difficult.
- Just as the Israelites were oppressed by the Midianites in Gideon's time, inflationary pressure robs us in the sense that the money we earn now has far less buying power.
- Many Bible scholars believe that the black horse described in Revelation chapter 6 personifies the economic hardship and inflationary pressure that will arise in the global economic system in the last days. In this passage, the scales of the rider represent the scales that are were used in the public marketplace and the rider proclaims that a quart of wheat will cost a day's wages, implying inflationary pressure (see Prov. 11:1 below).
- Regardless of the economic pressures we face, God is still Jehovah Jireh, which means *the Lord is my Provider.* He will provide for His people and help them to plan and prepare for times of trouble because He is faithful to His promises.

## Key Scriptures to Read and Pray Through

"Dishonest scales *are* an abomination to the Lord, but a just weight *is* His delight."—Proverbs 11:1

"And my God shall supply all your need according to His riches in glory by Christ Jesus."—Philippians 4:19

## Prayer Strategies

"Father, give us the insight and strategy we need to endure challenging economic times and plan effectively for them. Grant us the wisdom and the resolve to respond to Your words appropriately."

## 5

"There is coming a naval conflict in the South China Sea, which will cause the world markets to plummet. China will be involved and might claim it was an accident. The U.S. will be affected by this and will be in the middle of this growing China-Taiwan conflict."

## FULFILLMENT: Partial / Precursor Events Unfolding

### What has already happened to fulfill this word?

- China claims Taiwan as part of its territory, and while the U.S. recognizes the "One-China" policy, it opposes any attempt to change Taiwan's status by force (Richard, 2023).
- China has escalated tensions with Taiwan by deploying nearly two dozen warplanes and warships near Taiwan's territory. In one week, China flew over 150 warplanes toward Taiwan (Hagstrom, 2023).
- During diplomatic meetings this year, China also told the U.S., "It is necessary to make a choice between dialogue and confrontation, cooperation or conflict." China's foreign officials have said that the communist regime will not compromise or concede regarding Taiwan (Kent, 2023).

### What has not yet happened?

China has persistently provoked Taiwan while asserting its territorial claim over the island. Nevertheless, a unique and unprecedented naval conflict in the South China Sea has yet to unfold. Given our current President's weakness in foreign policy at the time of writing, it is likely this conflict will unfold in the very near future.

# War, Rumors of War, and the Future of the Chinese Communist Party

*by Michael Fickess*

**"You will hear of wars and rumors of wars. See that you are not troubled; for all *these things* must come to pass, but the end is not yet."—Matthew 24:6**

In Matthew 24, Jesus warned of wars as one of the signs of the end of the age. Since the world has always had wars and the context this warning appears in is a list of signs that increase in severity and frequency, we can interpret Christ's words to be a warning of *more frequent* and *more severe* wars unfolding as we approach the end of the age. In fact, the two World Wars of the last century and the Global War against Terrorism in the 21st century are most likely the beginning of the fulfillment of Christ's words.

Many have overlooked that Christ warned about "rumors of war." With "rumors of war," rising tensions present serious problems for nations even long before a shot is fired. While a hot war has obvious and immediate impacts on the people and the infrastructure, "rumors of war" have more subtle effects that can be just as devastating in the long term. The best example of this is in the Cold War between the United States and the Soviet Union, when rising tensions from a decades-long "rumor of war" had wide impacts on many nations around the globe, resulting in a series of proxy wars. Today, the conflict between China and Western nations has become a new Cold War, with China supporting terrorism behind the scenes and funneling weapons to our enemies—while robbing us with its currency manipulation.

When a war between China and Taiwan finally erupts in the South China Sea, it will be tempting to view this conflict as an expression of China's stature as a rising superpower with an ambition to take over the globe. However, the opposite is more likely the case—as Chris indicated in his prophecy about the downfall of President Xi, a new revolution is coming in China. And it is likely that China's aggression in the South China Sea will be Xi's last act of desperation before he is deposed by his own people. The devastating impacts of Western sanctions on an already fragile Chinese economy is likely to push the people over the edge, from discontentment to open revolt, resulting in a more free nation that can champion the gospel of Jesus Christ in the end times. In other words, a conflict in the South China Sea is something that God may use to accomplish a much greater purpose in mainland China and throughout all of Asia.

When Jesus warned of "wars and rumors of wars," he added the instruction: "see to it that you are not troubled." Hopefully, the historical perspective shared here will build faith and confidence in God's greater plan as He works through everything that will unfold through this future conflict.

# Key Scriptures to Read and Pray Through

*Since Taiwan is an island, we have highlighted key promises in scripture for "the islands of the sea" for declaration over Taiwan:*

"It shall come to pass in that day that the Lord shall set His hand again the second time to recover the remnant of His people who are left, from Assyria and Egypt, from Pathros and Cush, from Elam and Shinar, from Hamath and the islands of the sea."—Isaiah 11:11

Ask the Lord to draw Taiwan back to Himself.

"So when this was done, the rest of those on the island who had diseases also came and were healed."—Acts 28:9

Ask the Lord to release His healing power on the believers in Taiwan so that the gospel will spread through the whole region in the decades to come.

"I, John, both your brother and companion in the tribulation and kingdom and patience of Jesus Christ, was on the island that is called Patmos for the word of God and for the testimony of Jesus Christ. I was in the Spirit on the Lord's Day, and I heard behind me a loud voice, as of a trumpet…" —Revelation 1:9-10

Ask the Lord to reveal Himself supernaturally to the people of Taiwan just as He has revealed Himself as the "man in white" to Muslims throughout the Middle East, leading many thousands to put their faith in Christ.

## 6

"Gas prices are down temporarily
but will go back up."

**FULFILLMENT: Partly Fulfilled / Precursors Evident**

## What has already happened to fulfill this word?

- Gas prices surged by almost 11% in August, affecting the economy. However, a major blow at the pump could come as a result of the ongoing war in Israel. Analysts warn that if Iran enters the fray, it may trigger a surge in oil prices (Frazin, 2023).
- Under the Biden administration, the United States has drastically reduced its oil production, shifting us from energy independence to a deep reliance on other nations. This sets us up for more dramatic spikes in energy prices in the future (Robertson, 2023).

## What has not yet happened?

While gas prices currently remain below summer 2022 peaks, we await the expected rise in oil prices as a fulfillment of this word. It is likely that the unfolding Israel-Hamas War in the Middle East may contribute to a significant disruption in the oil supply, leading to the fulfillment of this word.

## Biblical Principles Related to this Word

- Scripture commands us to be self-sufficient if possible when it comes to our practical needs. This is why 2 Thessalonians 3:10 commands us: **"If anyone will not work, neither shall he eat."** The same is true on the national level: if we have the capacity to meet our own energy requirements and become self-sufficient, then it is foolish to do otherwise. Praying for the prices to go down without bothering to start drilling again is like a farmer praying for corn before he plants any seed: let's begin our prayers by asking God to give us righteous leaders who know how to properly steward the rich resources that He has already put in our land.

- An energy crisis is the modern equivalent of a famine because the bulk of our food and retail products are either made with oil, shipped with oil, or both. Just as God told Joseph to store up grain for the time of famine, wise national leaders will store up oil to prepare for shortages. Unfortunately, the current administration has chosen to use up a large percentage of the United States' strategic oil reserves for short-term political gains. This makes us far more vulnerable in the future.

## Key Scriptures to Read and Pray Through

Sometimes, the Lord gives us unique strategies to pray through. While the parable of the virgins is obviously about believers who prepare for the Lord's return by being filled with the anointing of the Spirit, it may be used in a different way here.

Read the parable of the wise and foolish virgins in Matthew 25: 1-13 as a parable about nations who store up *crude oil* so that they can thrive and spread the gospel in the darkest of times. Nations that literally "store up oil" will prosper and have the capacity to minister more effectively to impoverished nations.

**7**

"Crime will get worse. Rioting will hit the streets again, and people who are unhappy and fed up with their government not protecting its citizens will engage in serious protests."

## FULFILLMENT: Partly Fulfilled

## What has already happened to fulfill this word?

- In San Francisco, 97% of restaurants grapple with vandalism, compelling restaurateurs to incur substantial expenses for graffiti removal and window repairs. (Koeing, 2023).
- The crime rate in Democrat-run Chicago surged by 97% during the initial 22 days of 2023 when contrasted with the corresponding time frame in 2021. (Nolte, 2023).
- Hundreds of Oakland, California, residents demanded the city take action on the rising crime rates during a community safety meeting with local officials, with one resident saying they are the "victims of a failed progressive utopia" (Dixon-Hamilton, 2023).
- "Flash mob" looting has become more common. For example, in Philadelphia, thieves looted numerous stores after coordinating a mob on social media. Over 50 arrests were made, and extensive property damage occurred, including multiple liquor store break-ins (Associated Press, 2023).
- It has become clear that certain crime policies have caused unrest and a surge in crime in some states and cities.

# What has not yet happened?

While there have been many riots throughout the year, we have not yet seen riots that specifically protest the U.S. government's failure to protect its citizenry. Presumably, this specific kind of protest would be in response to the kinds of terrorism and incursion warned about in the Southern Border Dreams section of this book.

## Biblical Principles and Prayer Strategies

- Psalm 11:3 laments, **"If the foundations are destroyed, what can the righteous do?"** The only way to fix the issue of rising crime is to restore the foundations. The law of Moses is the foundation of modern government and contains all of the basic laws to create and maintain a civilized society. Likewise, Judeo-Christian values are the foundation of any healthy and thriving civilization. The reason for increasing lawlessness is rooted in our national failure to adhere to the Judeo-Christian foundations we have inherited. Pray that America would return to its righteous foundations, beginning with the basic enforcement of law and order in cases of violent crimes.

- *Read and pray through Psalm 11 in full: it laments the rise of wickedness, promises that the Lord sees all, and proclaims our fixed gaze upon the Lord, in whom we put all of our trust.*

- *Read and pray through Psalm 91 as a set of promises for your home, your work place, and your house of worship.*

- *Read and pray through Psalm 3 as a declaration of the Lord as your shield and defense who will protect you from the violence of widespread criminality and civil unrest.*

**8**

"Revealing the drastic divide between the Left Coast and Middle America, we will see bizarre weather extremes which will be blamed on climate change. We will see extreme fires in the Western U.S. and extreme flooding in the Eastern U.S."

## FULFILLMENT: Fulfilled, but Likely More to Come

## What has already happened to fulfill this word?

- This prophetic word has come to pass as Maui fires ravaged the western U.S., while Hurricane Idalia unleashed flooding on the eastern seaboard. In August 2023, the Hawaiian island of Maui on the western side of the United States was ravaged by the most devastating wildfire in the U.S. in a century (Salahieh, 2023). During that same month, Idalia, a category 3 hurricane, tore into Florida bringing major flooding and significant damage to the U.S. (Spencer, 2023).
- New York City experienced extreme flooding and broke historical records when over seven inches of rain fell on the region in less than 24 hours. The deluge shut down subways and "turned streets into rivers" (NBC, 2023).
- In responding to these natural disasters, U.S. President Joe Biden blamed climate change (Reuters, 2023).

### More Fulfillments Ahead?

While this word has technically already been fulfilled, it is likely to be a prophetic and meteorological pattern that either continues or increases in severity in the years to come because the "drastic divide" in American values is becoming more severe, not less severe, over time.

# Biblical Principles and Prayer Strategies

- As a "sign prophecy," this prophetic word is not really about *the weather,* but about a *national division* between those who hold traditional Biblical values and those who have abandoned this inheritance. The weather merely serves as a sign to draw our attention to this division, as indicated by the way the Lord presented this word to Chris.

- Not all divisions are bad. Jesus said, **"I did not come to bring peace but a sword. For I have come to 'set a man against his father, a daughter against her mother…'" (Matthew 10:34).** The reality is that the values and the culture of those who serve God will never be able to merge with the values and culture of the godless. This is why Paul tells us to **"have no fellowship with the unfruitful works of darkness" (Ephesians 5:11).** Yet, we are not without hope: the best way to reconcile our nation and heal our cultural divisions is to earnestly pray for a national spiritual awakening that brings man back to the Lord.

- The same Jesus who said **"Peace! Be Still!"** to the raging storm lives in us (Mark 4:39). Catastrophic weather arises for the same reason that illness and disease arise—for all of creation is under the curse of sin and death. When we pray for creation, our prayers are rooted in the atonement of Jesus Christ, who shed His blood not only to forgive our sins and heal our diseases but also to restore creation and remove the curse from it entirely. As priests of God under the New Covenant, we have been granted the authority to administrate the power of the blood of Christ to heal both mankind and the whole of creation.

**9**

"I saw a significant-sized building being damaged
by extreme wind or a weather phenomenon
which caused its crumbling and collapsing.
This will be a major news story.
This could happen in the Northeastern U.S."

## FULFILLMENT: Not Fulfilled

## How have we handled this word?

- We released an *MSJN Special Alert* about Hurricane Lee and the Atlantic hurricane season in general this year, warning of potentially severe impacts from Hurricane Lee and the other storms that followed in its wake. Using all of the prophetic insight and meteorological data available to us, our team warned people of potential impacts from the storm out of an abundance of caution—but we also internally wondered if it was possible that an Atlantic storm might fulfill this ominous warning word about a large building "crumbling and collapsing."

- We believe that the mobilization of intercession during Atlantic hurricane season was largely responsible for the lessening of this season's severity. While the rain fell in record amounts in some places, the most severe winds generally remained out at sea. For this reason, we also hold out hope that the fulfillment of this word about a wind-damaged building collapsing may have been averted by prayer this year—or perhaps that it will be averted in the future as we continue to pray intensively about every wind storm that targets the Northeastern United States.

# Biblical Principles and Prayer Strategies

- We are not in the business of blaming the victims of disaster: just as most sicknesses are not judgments from God, most natural disasters and catastrophes are not judgments from God. Rather, the general difficulties in love, both mundane and severe, arise from the curse of sin and death which is still at work in the world around us, affecting both the wicked and the righteous. This is why Jesus explained,

> **"He makes His sun rise on the evil and on the good, and sends rain on the just and on the unjust" (Matthew 5:45).**

*Ask the Lord to begin raising up relief workers to bring aid to those in need and the hope that only the gospel can bring before this or other disasters unfold.*

- In many cases, the occurrence of a significant disaster at a symbolic place serves as a sign prophecy, as discussed in the introduction to this book. For example, the Islamic terrorists intentionally targeted the Pentagon and the World Trade Center because they symbolized America's military strength and economic power. This clear symbolism is worth noting because it helps us to understand what the enemy is targeting or what the Lord is seeking to expose or restore. As a Biblical example, the destruction of the temple in Jerusalem, both at the time of the Babylonian captivity and in 70 A.D. served as a clear symbol of God's judgment because the temple symbolized the national identity as a "kingdom of priests" which they rejected when they turned towards idolatry.

*When an event like this happens, join with a local prayer group to ask the Lord what He is saying through it. Interpret the event as you would interpret a prophecy to develop a clear plan for how to pray about what is unfolding.*

- There is a subtle indication in this prophecy that this tower falling will indeed be symbolic in nature because there is likely a reason that it may happen *"…in the Northeast"*—for this region is the place of America's founding, the place where the Puritans first landed seeking religious freedom in 1620 and where the Declaration of Independence was signed in 1776. A tower falling in this region may well be a symbolic representation of our departure from the national roots of religious liberty and freedom from governmental tyranny.

*Pray that the Lord will move in the Northeast and bring the American people back to Himself.*

- Intellectualism is a stronghold in the Northeast, but when difficult events happen that defy reason, it can often break people out of a pattern of intellectualism, forcing them to seek spiritual answers when rational answers are no longer available. Many people respond to disaster by questioning God, but this line of questioning can often lead to a sustained season of people actually *returning* to God if handled properly. This is why the prophet Hosea declared:

**¹ Come, and let us return to the Lord;**
**For He has torn, but He will heal us;**
**He has stricken, but He will bind us up.**

**² After two days He will revive us;**
**On the third day He will raise us up,**
**That we may live in His sight.**

**³ Let us know, let us pursue the knowledge of the Lord.**
**His going forth is established as the morning;**
**He will come to us like the rain,**
**Like the latter *and* former rain to the earth.**
**—Hosea 6:1-3**

This passage in Hosea promises a season of seeking the Lord, restoration and renewal that may follow in the wake of disaster. But in order to see this redemptive process unfold, the Body of Christ must first mobilize to bring relief to victims, evangelize in an appropriate and effective way, and minister to the hurting as the Spirit leads.

*Pray that the Lord will "send workers for the Harvest" when hard times unfold.*

*Pray that instead of having their hearts hardened, the American people will discern the Lord's hand in what unfolds so that they will return to Him.*

**10**

"In the middle of rising gas prices, I saw a costly oil spill in the Southeastern United States. I saw oil-saturated beaches in Florida. This will be a difficult challenge for Governor Ron DeSantis to navigate. This will be a third test for him, and he will have a literal mess on his hands. Please pray for him in this situation."

## FULFILLMENT: Not Yet Fulfilled

## What has not yet happened?

• This specific word has not happened yet.   However, there is ample precedent for oil spills, both off the Alaskan coast and in the Gulf of Mexico because the maritime routes for oil tankers pass through these waters frequently.

• This word is also likely related to prophetic word #6 which predicts rising gas prices because the context given is that this will be, "in the middle of rising gas prices…"  This suggests that we should be more watchful over this particular word when the warning of rising energy costs comes to pass.

## Biblical Principles Related to this Word

• God prepared King David to be king by allowing him to face a series of challenges: as a shepherd, he faced the lion and the bear to prepare him to confront Goliath.  The defeat of Goliath prepared him to face even greater battles in the years that followed.  As a leader, every trial he faced was designed by God to develop him as an effective leader of the nation.  Likewise, let us pray that the Lord uses this event—and other events in Governor DeSantis' life—to make him the leader that God has called him to become.

## Prayer Strategies

- God spoke through the prophet Samuel that David was, **"a man after his own heart" (1 Samuel 13:14).** In the same way, pray that the Holy Spirit will work in Governor Ron DeSantis, granting him the courage he needs to stand for righteousness and the wisdom he needs to navigate new challenges in each season of his public service.

## Key Passage to Pray Through

¹ I will lift up my eyes to the hills—
From whence comes my help?

² My help *comes* from the Lord,
Who made heaven and earth.

³ He will not allow your foot to be moved;
He who keeps you will not slumber.

⁴ Behold, He who keeps Israel
Shall neither slumber nor sleep.

⁵ The Lord *is* your keeper;
The Lord *is* your shade at your right hand.

⁶ The sun shall not strike you by day,
Nor the moon by night.

⁷ The Lord shall preserve you from all evil;
He shall preserve your soul.

⁸ The Lord shall preserve your going out and your coming in
from this time forth, and even forevermore.

—Psalm 121:1-8

## 11

"I had a unique vision, twice confirmed, of an airplane that mysteriously disappeared in the skies like the Indonesian flight a few years ago. This plane will carry sensitive intelligence information. Its mysterious disappearance will make the news, then it will reappear or be found."

## FULFILLMENT: Fulfilled Precisely

## What has already happened to fulfill this word?

- A missing F-35 fighter jet in South Carolina was reported by all mainstream news sites. Joint Base Charleston confirmed that the pilot ejected after the plane suffered an unspecified mishap.

- Authorities located the aircraft's debris after more than a day of searching, and they dispatched teams to secure the wreckage and conduct an investigation (Copp, 2023).

- Advanced stealth technology is one of the U.S. government's best-kept and carefully guarded secrets, so the disappearance of this fighter most certainly qualifies as "sensitive intelligence information," leading to a precise fulfillment of this prophetic word.

# Biblical Principles Related to this Word

- Whether we are talking about an airplane or your missing car keys, there is biblical precedent for the Lord helping us to find lost things. In 2 Kings 5, the company of prophets was devastated when an axe-head turned up missing. However, a man of God caused the axe-head to float by the power of the Spirit. Likewise, God will intervene when we ask him to.

*While this word has already been precisely fulfilled, it is also possible that it may recur: if another plane is lost with valuable assets, we will have another opportunity to pray.*

- Scripture does record judgments in some cases for leaders who betray their nation or divulge intelligence information. For example, Hezekiah was rebuked by a prophet of the Lord when he revealed all of the treasure rooms in Israel to envoys from Babylon (see the full story in Isaiah chapter 39). While the location and the amount of treasure should have been kept secret, Hezekiah compromised ancient Israel's national security by revealing this privileged information to the enemy. Likewise, our military secrets are as valuable as national treasure and must be closely guarded, especially in times of increasing conflict around the globe. The disappearance of this plane could well be a "sign prophecy" that warns us to guard our national secrets more carefully because of heightened risks.

*Pray that the Lord will raise up responsible leaders in the U.S. government and U.S. military who will take their sacred trust to defend our nation seriously.*

*Pray that our leaders will be sober-minded and careful when dealing with representatives or agents from other nations.*

## 12

"As part of the major flooding in the Eastern U.S., I saw a dam burst which caused even more severe flooding. This will be a natural sign of another dam about to break in government corruption and lies, which also can no longer be contained."

## FULFILLMENT: Partial, Precursor Patterns

## What has already happened to fulfill this word?

- Although not a direct fulfillment of this word, it is notable that this year saw two neglected dams in northeast Libya break, unleashing a devastating flood in Derna. Over 5,000 people are believed to have been killed with thousands more missing. The flood resulted from Storm Daniel, which brought extreme rainfall to Libya (Paddison, 2023).
- As another precursor patter, a flood in India's Himalayan northeast, triggered by a glacial lake overflow, destroyed a major hydroelectric dam, killing 31 people, displacing thousands, and raising concerns about dam safety (VOA News, 2023).
- With allegations surrounding the Biden family's financial dealings and the White House deflecting accusations, it seems that "the corruption dam" is indeed about to break for Joe Biden (Devine, 2023).

## What has not yet happened?

We have yet to witness a major dam breaking in the United States since this word was prophesied and the full extent of the Biden family's corruption remains to be revealed, awaiting the moment when the flood of truth washes away the dam of lies.

## Biblical Principles and Prayers

Dams and walls are very similar in their symbolic value. For example, just as a well-built wall can hold back enemies that might otherwise destroy a city, a well-built dam can hold back the waters that might otherwise flood a low-lying region. In both cases, the integrity of the structure must be maintained because any weakness will be exploited. Likewise, leaders who have trafficked in corruption and lies may feel certain that they have built up strong defenses against ever being exposed and that there will be no "leaks" about what they have done. But for the greater good of the nation, the Lord will cause this false security to fall apart.

*Ask the Father to expose lies and reveal corruption so that a wave of reformation, renewal and repentance can sweep through the United States government.*

*Ask the Lord to "take the death out" of any potential disasters involving a collapsed dam, so that there will be no serious human casualties—even when the Lord allows the dam to break as a "sign prophecy" indicating His plans.*

## Key Scriptures to Read and Pray Through

**"And He will bring down their pride
together with the trickery of their hands.**

**"The fortress of the high fort of your walls
He will bring down, lay low, and bring to the ground,
down to the dust."—Isaiah 25:11b-12**

**13**

"The 'Ronald-Donald' battle. I saw in a vision Donald Trump and Ron DeSantis battling it out for the Republican presidential nomination. A nasty battle will unfold in the primaries. Trump will accuse DeSantis of not being loyal to him and will express betrayal because DeSantis refused to bow out, just so he can have another run at Trump. Just when it looks like DeSantis is creeping ahead of Trump, dirt will be dug up and cold evidence will be used against him. I saw this in a news headline. Despite this, Ron DeSantis will become a leader in Washington D.C. and a future President of the United States."

## FULFILLMENT: Partly Fulfilled

## What has already happened to fulfill this word?

- Donald Trump started criticizing DeSantis personally as "disloyal and ungrateful" even before the Florida Governor announced his candidacy for the 2024 presidential election. Trump is also attacking DeSantis for his policies on issues like Social Security and Medicare (Reid, 2023).

- DeSantis has started directly criticizing Trump's unfulfilled promises during campaign speeches, signaling a shift in the Republican race (Nehamas, 2023).

- In recent polls, Donald Trump's support among potential GOP primary voters has reached record highs, while Ron DeSantis is trailing behind (Yokley, 2023).

## What has not yet happened?

We have not yet seen significant scandals—or even accusations of scandals—involving Governor Ron DeSantis. The reference to "digging up dirt" on DeSantis suggests that Trump will hire staff to conduct opposition research on DeSantis, a common political tactic often used late in campaigns to attack an opponent's character or past choices. It is too early to judge the second half of this prophecy, which projects Ron DeSantis as a "future president."

## Biblical Principles and Prayer Strategies

While some political competition can be healthy in an election, the in-fighting among Republican primary candidates can have long-term negative impacts on whichever candidate ultimately becomes the Republican nominee for President in 2024.

*Pray that all of the Republican primary candidates—including Trump and DeSantis—will shift their focus from attacking one another to criticizing the destructive policies of the Biden administration.*

*Pray for the winner of the Republican nomination to have a clear message of reformation going into the 2024 election that will reunite those who are divided in the conservative movement.*

## Key Scriptures to Read and Pray Through

**"But if you bite and devour one another, beware lest you be consumed by one another!"—Galatians 5:15**

**"Every kingdom divided against itself is brought to desolation, and every city or house divided against itself will not stand."—Matthew 12:25**

**14**

"I also saw a woman of color, which I predicted last year. I do not know her ethnicity, but a woman of color will carry a word and will carry Trump to the top of the ticket and help restore his credibility which was lost with voters over the last two years. This woman of color will come alongside him and bring to light the corruption in social media and the American election system. She will help vindicate his claims of election fraud."

## FULFILLMENT: Not Yet Fulfilled

☐

## What has already happened to fulfill this word?

- Nikki Haley, former UN Ambassador during the Trump Administration and child of Indian immigrants, announced her bid for the 2024 Republican presidential nomination, becoming the first woman of color to be a major contender in this race (Thomson-DeVeaux, 2023).

- Other notable women of color, such as media figure Candace Owens of *The Daily Wire* and Virginia Lt. Gov. Winsome Earle-Sears who was part of a dramatic re-shaping of Virginia politics, are some of the larger pool of figures who may be related to the future fulfillment of this word.

## What has not yet happened?

It remains a mystery exactly who will be the woman of color that 'comes alongside' Trump to help him restore his credibility.

## Biblical Principles Related to this Word

In Scripture, the spirit of Wisdom is uniquely described and personified as a woman (see Proverbs 1:20-21). In addition to benefitting from the support of a specific person, this could suggest that Trump also needs much more *Wisdom* in order to avoid making the kinds of mistakes that could cost him an election victory in 2024.

*Pray that the Lord grants more Wisdom to President Trump, his future running mate, and his advisors on the campaign.*

*Pray that the spirit of Wisdom will prevent Trump and his team from making foolish or costly mistakes in the presidential campaign.*

## Key Passage to Read and Pray Through

**20 Wisdom calls aloud outside;**
**She raises her voice in the open squares.**

**21 She cries out in the chief concourses,**
**At the openings of the gates in the city**
**She speaks her words:**

**22 "How long, you simple ones, will you love simplicity?**
**For scorners delight in their scorning,**
**And fools hate knowledge.**

**23 "Turn at my rebuke;**
**Surely I will pour out my spirit on you;**
**I will make my words known to you."**

**—Proverbs 1:20-23**

## 15

**(A)** "Chinese influence and bribery will be exposed, and it will be shocking how much China's tentacles have reached into many nations around the world. This will include American politics and helping to swing the 2020 election. This will come to light, will be undeniable and will again be tied to the Hunter Biden laptop scandal, which will be fully exposed and tie Joe Biden to everything."

**(B)** "Three times, I saw boxes being opened and I saw the words "smoking gun," which will prove beyond a doubt Chinese money and involvement in Biden's campaign and secrets being exposed even through the courts and House of Representatives. This will shock the world. Remember: boxes, Biden, and billionaires. Even suppression, manipulation, and intimidation in our courts will be exposed, revealing they knew more than what they were willing to say."

## FULFILLMENT: Mostly Fulfilled with Precision

## What has already happened to fulfill this word?

- Banking records and laptop data have revealed Hunter Biden's dealings with a Chinese Energy Company. Hunter and his uncle, James Biden, received nearly five million dollars as a payment for Hunter's services (Viser, 2023).
- A case that became public knowledge on January 9, 2023, revealed an ongoing investigation about classified documents linked to President Biden's tenures as senator and vice president.

- In November 2022, documents were discovered at the Penn Biden Center in Washington, D.C., prompting an investigation into the mishandling of classified documents by Joe Biden.
- Additional classified documents were found at Biden's Delaware residence in December 2022. Biden claimed to be unaware of the document's contents (Doherty, 2023).
- In January 2023, there was an additional search of Biden's Delaware residence and classified documents were discovered in Biden's Delaware garage near his Corvette (Nelson, 2023).
- After the case was public, House Committee Chair Comer requested UPenn to disclose anonymous Chinese donations of millions of dollars to the Penn Biden Center, citing concerns about the discovery of classified documents in that location (Nava, 2023).

## What has not yet happened?

- While the classified document boxes found at Biden's home and affiliated offices suggest profound governmental corruption, their contents remain undisclosed to the public. This means that part of this prophecy remains unfulfilled, but will presumably come to fruition when the contents of these documents are more fully disclosed.

- While connections between Chinese officials and the Biden family have been proven, the evidence for Chinese influence on the 2020 election has not yet been fully brought into the light.

## Key Scripture to Read and Pray Through

*"For nothing is secret that will not be revealed, nor anything hidden that will not be known and come to light."*—Luke 8:17

## 16

"As predicted last year, I saw food shortages in 2023.
This will be a year of revolution around the world.
Third world countries, Mexico, and South America
will be hit hardest by food chain and
food supply shortages."

## FULFILLMENT: Partly Fulfilled

## What has already happened to fulfill this word?

- The impact of Russia's invasion of Ukraine has been felt across the world. The Russian-Ukraine war has impacted food supply, shortage of consumer products, and inflation, especially in third-world countries (Kozul-Wright, 2023).

- According to the World Bank, the global food crisis worsened in 2023 due to rising food price inflation, conflicts, economic challenges, and climate-related issues, affecting especially third-world countries (World Bank, 2023).

- India halted non-basmati white rice exports to stabilize domestic prices (Jha, 2023).

- A confluence of extreme weather conditions, export curbs, and geopolitical tensions poses risks to food availability and security in developing countries with less production capabilities, thus fulfilling Chris' prophecy.

## What has not yet happened?

While there have been countless riots and protests around the world in 2023, most of these have not yet progressed into the full-scale revolutions that this word warns about in response to food shortages.

## Biblical Principles and Prayer Strategies

- Famines do not occur in a vacuum—they arise as the result of deeper systemic problems. For example, famines may happen when wars destabilize nations, when extreme weather such as drought or flood reduces a harvest, or when regimes compound found shortages through corruption and mismanagement. Often, we need to dig deeper when we're praying about a famine to look for the root cause and pray about that first.

*Focus on one nation or region of the world and ask the Father to deal with the systemic problems in that region that have caused food shortages or increased poverty.*

- The Lord cares deeply for those who suffer from hunger and poverty. Jesus taught that at the final judgment, those who fed the hungry would be rewarded as if they fed Jesus himself. Likewise, those who did not feed the hungry will be condemned as if they neglected Jesus (Matthew 25:31-46)

*It is not enough to simply pray that God will feed the hungry—he requires us to step up in concerted ways. Consider donating to a local food pantry or giving funds to a trusted charity that feeds the hungry in America or abroad.*

**17**

"I saw a worsening immigration problem across our Southern border. The illegal immigrant situation will culminate in an epic border crisis/showdown."

## FULFILLMENT: Partially Fulfilled

## What has already happened to fulfill this word?

- Illegal crossings along the U.S. southern border jumped more than 30% in July with U.S. agents making more than 130,000 arrests along the Mexico border (Miroff, 2023).

- In August, a record 91,000 migrant families crossed the U.S.-Mexico border, exceeding the previous monthly record. Unaccompanied minors also increased. The rise in illegal crossings coincides with the revelation that officials welded open gates along the Arizona border to allow water flow during the monsoon season (Koenig, 2023).

- *Additional information about the border crisis and the heightened risks of terrorism that arise from an unguarded border is listed in Appendix 1 of this book.*

## What has not yet happened?

We stand at a critical point in the southern border issue, witnessing a significant surge in illegal border crossings in 2023. Yet, an impending "epic border crisis/showdown," which presumably would involve a much larger mobilization of border agents, law enforcement, or military units, has not yet occurred.

# Balancing God's Heart for Immigration with Security Threats at the Southern Border

*by Michael Fickess*

America has often been called a "nation of immigrants." Our history of immigration from around the world has made our nation stronger. Our nation's general attitude towards immigration is best summarized by the plaque at the base of the Statue of Liberty, which reads:

> *"Give me your tired, your poor,*
> *Your huddled masses yearning to breathe free,*
> *The wretched refuse of your teeming shore.*
> *Send these, the homeless, tempest-tossed to me,*
> *I lift my lamp beside the golden door!"*

Despite our national heart of compassion and our historical place as a beacon of freedom and opportunity for nations around the world, we must draw a distinction between (a) groups of legal immigrants who come to America in search of liberty and opportunity and (b) illegal immigrants who are going through no security screening or vetting process.

While legal immigrants can be properly screened and welcomed when they have noble intentions, illegal immigration is a major problem because it allows millions to enter the United States without any security screening at all. This provides cover for terrorists and criminal gang members such as Mexican cartel operatives or MS-13.

In order to gain a strong Biblical perspective on this issue, we have to apply different Biblical principles to each group. First, we have a Biblical mandate to be hospitable and kind to the legal immigrants who come to our nation for political asylum, religious freedom, liberty, and economic opportunity. Consider how the Bible commands us to treat immigrants in the following verses:

**"You shall also love the stranger, for you were strangers in the land of Egypt."—Deuteronomy 10:19**

**"The alien who resides with you shall be to you as the citizen among you; you shall love the alien as yourself, for you were aliens in the land of Egypt: I am the Lord your God."**
— Leviticus 19:34

**"Cursed is anyone who withholds justice from the foreigner, the fatherless or the widow."—Deuteronomy 27:19**

**"I was hungry and you gave me food, I was thirsty and you gave me drink, I was a stranger and you welcomed me."**
**—Matthew 25:35**

It is clear from scripture that God commands us not only to treat immigrants with justice but also to *love* them and to express that love with acts of charity. However, none of these Biblical mandates apply to those who come illegally and with the intention of doing harm to our nation, our people, or our way of life. In fact, the terrorists, Mexican cartel members, or gang members who pose as "immigrants" would be more accurately categorized as *enemy combatants* and should be treated as such. For the *enemy combatants* that cross our border, the scriptures paint an entirely different picture of how they should be treated:

**"But if you do evil, be afraid; for he does not bear the sword in vain; for he is God's minister, an avenger to *execute* wrath on him who practices evil."—Romans 13:4**

The Bible does not advocate pacifism when it comes to dealing with serious evil and criminal behavior. Rather, there is a clear Biblical mandate for the government to establish law and order and enforce its laws by any means necessary—including capital punishment.

If we want to see a vision of what perfect government looks like, we need to look at New Jerusalem as it is described in Revelation 21 and 22. It is a city that the Lord calls His Bride. There is no curse of sin and death there and everything shines with the glory of God continually. Yet, even the New Jerusalem is a city with walls and gates. And there is also a host of people whom God does not let into His city because they did not pass his rigorous vetting process:

**"But outside *are* dogs and sorcerers and sexually immoral and murderers and idolaters, and whoever loves and practices a lie."—Revelation 22:14-15**

In order to pray about this issue effectively and talk about it with moral clarity, we need to take the time to draw these distinctions, being careful to show love and kindness to the immigrants that cross our path, while also advocating for strong walls, guarded gates, and swift punishment upon the evil-doers among us.

*For additional insight into this particular word, see the prophetic warning dreams shared by Chris Reed and Rick Joyner, as well as the documentation from our MSJN team in Appendix 1 of this book.*

## Prayer Strategies

- Ask the Lord to release a spirit of wisdom, revelation, and discernment on our border agents, intelligence agencies, and law enforcement so they can discern enemy intruders in our midst (Ephesians 1:17, 1 Peter 5:8).
- Ask the Lord to give moral clarity and biblical insight to leaders at the local level and the national level.

## 18

"I saw African nations experience severe food shortages and migrants coming to America not only from Central and South America but also from Africa and Europe."

## FULFILLMENT: Partially Fulfilled

## What has already happened to fulfill this word?

• The hunger crisis in the Horn of Africa has escalated to unprecedented levels, with 23 million people in Ethiopia, Kenya, and Somalia grappling with acute food insecurity and confronting dire shortages of both sustenance and clean water. (UNHCR, 2023).

• Food insecurity in West and Central Africa is now affecting 47.2 million people in this year's "lean season" which is when hunger usually peaks (Asadu, 2023).

## What has not yet happened?

In 2023, hunger surged in African nations, but a significant increase of migrants from Europe and Africa to America has yet to come to pass.

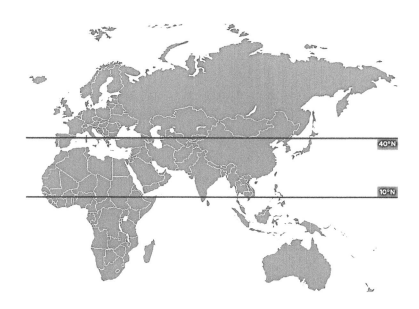

## Prayer Strategy—The 10/40 Window

The term 10/40 Window was first used in 1990 by Luis Bush. This describes the region between ten and forty degrees north latitude in which 90% of the world's unreached people groups reside. In the 1990's and the early 2000's, thousands of believers mobilized in prayer for those who live in these areas, softening the ground for evangelism and the discipling of nations. That prayer movement likely softened the ground for the accelerated growth of the underground church in China, Iran, Iraq, and other nations where believers are persecuted.

*One of the main reasons that nations experience severe food shortages is because of corrupt and oppressive governments and economies. Pray for government reform and economic reform.*

*Ask the Father to push back the darkness and shine the light of the gospel in this region.*

*Identify two or three missionaries to Africa, Europe, or Central and South America that you can pray for each day by name.*

73

**19**

"There will come a tipping point for the United States. Something—or someone—will cross the U.S. southern border, and when what they are doing is brought to light, it will be so terrible and horrendous that it will force both political parties to get aggressive in protecting our borders."

## FULFILLMENT: Mostly Fulfilled

## What has already happened to fulfill this word?

- There has been a significant increase in migrants whose identities match those in the Terrorist Screening Dataset that have been caught when crossing the southern border in 2023. (Ainsley, 20).

- Fentanyl seizures have increased significantly in fiscal year 2023 compared to previous years (Ballesteros, 2023).

- In a surprising reversal, President Biden approved the continuation of Trump's border wall, and even so-called 'sanctuary cities' have changed their approach to migrants. (Borelli, 2023). This is perhaps the very beginning of the political shift this prophetic word suggests.

*See Appendix 1 for a much full set of prophetic articles and documentation on serious risks of the border crisis.*

## What has not yet happened?

In spite of the Biden Administration's new plan to continue the southern border wall construction, we have yet to see both political parties truly "get aggressive in protecting our borders" due to a traumatic event at the southern border.

## Biblical Principles Related to this Word

The description of this threat as "terrible and horrendous" implies that it is driven by demonic powers or a demonic ideology. Whether these risks come from Islamic terrorism, Mexican cartels, or someone else, effective spiritual warfare through prayer, worship, and prophetic declaration can help to pave the way for intelligence agencies, border agents, and law enforcement to catch dangerous intruders who might otherwise move undetected.

*Pray specifically to bless our intelligence agencies, border agents, and police officers. Pray for quick discovery and apprehension of terrorists and criminal intruders at the border—or wherever they are hiding in America.*

## Prayer Strategies

In 2 Kings 6, Elisha and his servant Gehazi were completely surrounded by the enemy (the Arameans). However, when Gehazi's eyes were opened to see into the realm of the Spirit, he saw the hills around them are filled with angels. A dramatic victory over the Arameans came right after this encounter. There's an important lesson to be learned here: our victory over *very real* enemies begins with our ability to look at everything through a prophetic lens so that we can gain the understanding that God is still on the throne, He has a clear plan, and He is waiting for us to pray so that He can release many angels on our nation's behalf.

## 20

"I saw the January 6 Hearings, which are now wrapping up, will be seen as a clandestine operation from foreign money peddling and influence, particularly Chinese and Russian money. Even the courts will be challenged again for their manipulation and for blaming everything on Trump. They did this because their nations suffered from Trump's policies."

## FULFILLMENT: Not Yet Fulfilled

## What has not yet happened?

It is not unusual for circumstances to directly contradict a prophetic word in the season just before we reach its time of fulfillment. In this case, the exact opposite of what the word promises is happening—instead of President Trump being vindicated by the courts, he is currently undergoing a series of political prosecutions. However, this actually helps create the environment for a major turn-around in the legal battles surrounding the 2020 election and the events of January 6, 2021.

As the old expression goes, "What's good for the goose is good for the gander." The political prosecution of Trump and many of his allies *sets a precedent* of political prosecution in America that is nearly certain to go the other direction if more Republicans take office after the next election.

A good comparison for this word is to consider how the truth about the COVID-19 virus' origins in a Chinese weapons lab was covered up and squelched on the nightly news and on social media. Yet, the clear fact of its origin was later presented and accepted on most of the same outlets that rejected it at first.

## Biblical Principles Related to this Word

We are called to pray *against* the fulfillment of some prophetic words because they warn of an attack of the enemy, a disaster, or an accident that the Lord wants us to bind with His authority (Matthew 18:18). However, this particular prophetic word would involve an exposure of corruption and conspiracy that would have a dramatic and positive impact on the long-term path of the United States.

It is certain that the "powers that be," both in the government and in the spirit realm, would forcefully resist this level of exposure. For this reason, let us pray *for* the fulfillment of this word so that any works that remain in the darkness and hidden from the public will come to light.

## Key Scriptures to Read and Pray Through

**"Assuredly, I say to you,
whatever you bind on earth
will be bound in heaven,
and whatever you loose on earth
will be loosed in heaven."
—Matthew 18:18**

*Read Psalm 3 as a psalm of vindication for any conservative voices who have been targeted with political prosecutions.*

*Read Psalm 2 as a psalm about the Lord "laughing" at and disrupting the complex plans of the world's leaders*

## 21

"Joe Biden and Kamala Harris will not be the leading Democratic Party ticket in the next election cycle. I saw a man winning the Democratic nomination, but it was not Joe Biden."

## FULFILLMENT: Too early to judge

## What has already happened to fulfill this word?

- At the time of writing, President Biden holds the lowest approval rating compared to the Bush, Obama, and Trump administrations in the same period. (Real Clear Politics, 2023).

- It's not just a "Biden problem"—Kamala holds a lower approval rating than the president. According to a new poll from The Associated Press-NORC Center for Public Affairs Research, just 37% of Democrats say they want Biden to seek a second term, down from 52% in the weeks before the midterm elections (Boak, 2023).

- On the other hand, Gavin Newsom's declaration of not running for President contradicts his actions: meeting with influential Democratic groups nationwide, substantial fundraising and donations, and vocal opposition against Republicans. This sparks suspicion about his potential candidacy in the 2024 presidential elections (Lightman, 2023).

## What has not yet happened?

Although Democratic leadership staunchly supports Joe Biden, they acknowledge concerns about his advanced age and his disapproval rating.

## Biblical Principles Related to this Word

There are many different cases in the Bible where the Lord removes one leader to make room for a more righteous leader. The most well-known example of this in the Bible is when Saul was removed from power by God to make room for David, a "man after God's own heart," to become king.

## Key Scriptures to Read and Pray Through

**"And Samuel said to Saul, 'You have done foolishly. You have not kept the commandment of the Lord your God, which He commanded you. For now the Lord would have established your kingdom over Israel forever.**

**'But now your kingdom shall not continue. The Lord has sought for Himself a man after His own heart, and the Lord has commanded him *to be* commander over His people, because you have not kept what the Lord commanded you.'"—1 Samuel 13:13-14**

## Prayer Strategies

It is likely that most readers of this book plan on supporting the candidate in 2024 who is the strongest advocate for Biblical values and conservative governance. However, it is prudent (and Biblical) for us to pray fervently for the nominees of both major political parties. Pray that the nominees for both the Republican and the Democratic parties in 2024 will be "men after God's own heart" just as David was.

**22**

"I saw a revolution of unrest, upheaval, and violence happening in Sweden. Sudden acts of terrorism will take place involving guns against citizens, and it will be led by a demon of anarchy. Lawlessness and anger will cause certain individuals to harm and destroy lives. People will become angry over the massive illegal immigration in Europe. Racism will also be a motivating factor in this violence in Sweden. Terrorists are taking advantage of this worldwide immigration crisis."

## FULFILLMENT: Mostly Fulfilled

## What has already happened to fulfill this word?

- Sweden has experienced a surge in gang violence, with numerous fatal shootings. Even innocents are targeted, leading to growing fear and insecurity (Reed, 2023).

- The escalation in violent incidents has prompted a strong response from Prime Minister Ulf Kristersson, who addressed the nation. Kristersson announced a multi-faceted strategy to combat escalating gang violence, involving collaboration between the government, police and the military.

- This came after 12 people were killed in September 2023, the second deadliest month on record for gun crime in Sweden (Fleck, 2023).

- Statistics provided by the Swedish police showed 283 armed attacks between rival gangs recorded in 2023. The clashes have resulted in 44 fatalities and 87 injured, painting a grim picture of the ongoing gang warfare (Altunas, 2023).

## What has not yet happened?

We have yet to see unmistakable proof of racially motivated crime in Sweden amidst a severe surge in gang violence within the nation. We also have not yet seen, "terrorists taking advantage of this worldwide immigration crisis," although the conditions for a new wave of terrorism are in place now as a global jihadist response to the Israel-Hamas war.

## Biblical Principles Related to this Word

In the story of Cain and Abel, Cain was angry and murdered his brother because his sacrifice was not accepted (Genesis 4). In the same way, the demonic and murderous rage of Islamic jihadists is ultimately driven by the spiritual reality that their religious system is not acceptable to God. Just like Cain, the violence of jihadism flows from spiritual darkness and rejection.

*Pray for a divine turn-around in Europe so that instead of immigrants bringing false religion to oppress a historically Christian region, strong Christian movements will arise in Europe to bring Muslim immigrants to the saving knowledge, light, and peace that only Jesus Christ can bring.*

***Additional Prophetic Resource:*** *Bob Jones' 1994 prophecy for Russia also includes important prophetic insight for Europe. This full prophecy may be viewed at* www.MorningStarJournal.com/russia

## Key Scriptures to Read and Pray Through

**"Violence shall no longer be heard in your land,
Neither wasting nor destruction within your borders;
But you shall call your walls Salvation,
And your gates Praise."—Isaiah 60:18**

**23**

"I saw a new sense of patriotism in European nations—France, Denmark, Poland, Hungary, and Italy—where people will redevelop national pride and a love for country. Some nations will begin their own "Brexit" processes from the European Union."

## FULFILLMENT: Mostly Fulfilled

## What has already happened to fulfill this word?

- Nationalist, right wing parties are gaining support across Europe, driven by concerns related to Russia's war in Ukraine, the cost of living, and the COVID-19 pandemic.

- Backlash against immigration, LGBTQ rights, abortion, and support for Ukraine is evident through polls. These forces are positioning themselves as "conservative" and "patriotic" ahead of the next EU elections (Gosling, 2023).

- Hungary and Poland vetoed a European Union migration agreement, opposing mandatory migrant quotas. The move, largely symbolic, reflects ongoing divisions within the EU over migration policies (COOK, 2023).

- In France, President Macron struggled, while right-wing leader Marine Le Pen gained support. Italy's government has a God, family and country agenda, and right-wing nationalists joined Finland's coalition. Sweden's anti-immigrant party supports the right-wing coalition, and Greece has seen conservative parties enter parliament. Spain's Vox Party surged, potentially forming a coalition government. Even Germany's AfD has been competitive in polls (Adler, 2023).

# What has not yet happened?

Nationalism and patriotic fervor are on the rise across European nations. However, this growing trend could potentially lead some of these countries to seek secession from the European Union, fulfilling this prophecy.

## Biblical Principles Related to this Word

This prophecy is a redemptive promise with an important purpose: while the enemy desires to assimilate all nations into one globalized and oppressive system of darkness, God loves our national distinctions and the diversity of our languages and cultures. This is why scripture promises a great harvest of souls from many different distinct national identities and cultures in which these unique identities remain intact:

**"After these things I looked, and behold, a great multitude which no one could number, of all nations, tribes, peoples, and tongues, standing before the throne and before the Lamb..." (Revelation 7:9)**

Likewise, the Lord Jesus was extremely zealous about making sure that His Father's house would remain a **"house of prayer for all nations" (Mark 11:17)**. While the resurgence of nationalism has in some cases led to fascism, it can also be an important precursor for a harvest of souls in these nations.

## Prayer Strategies

- *Pray that these nationalist movements in Europe would include a return to Europe's early Christian roots so these movements become redemptive in their purpose.*
- *Pray for Europe to experience a revival that includes an outpouring of the Holy Spirit and the salvation of many souls.*

## 24

"I saw a housing and homelessness crisis increasing in Europe which will lead to instability, uncertainty, and fear in the hearts of many European nations. People will respond to this with national priorities and protests over immigration policies in Europe. The massive illegal immigration coming into Europe from the South will become unsustainable and European nations will demand their national borders be observed and patriotism will become a priority. This will set the stage for destabilization of the European Union, inflation, immigration, food shortages, and an economic downturn. This will cause unrest across Europe."

## FULFILLMENT: Fulfilled and Continuing

## What has already happened to fulfill this word?

- Europe faces a housing crisis with soaring rents, overcrowded conditions, and lack of affordable housing. Rising costs, external shocks, and low supply contribute to this worsening situation (York, 2023).
- Italy approved measures to address a surge in migration from Tunisia. Premier Giorgia Meloni has also suggested the possibility of a naval blockade in North Africa to counter human traffickers (The Associated Press, 2023).
- The UK Home Secretary, Suella Braverman, called for addressing the unsustainable global migration crisis, emphasizing the need to redefine legitimate asylum-seekers and advocating for changes in asylum procedures (Doornbos, 2023).
- Anti-immigrant protests have surged in Ireland, with right-wing groups claiming discrimination against indigenous Irish due to

immigration issues. This movement has seen a significant increase in 2023 (Askew, 2023).

- As Europe grapples with a mounting housing crisis and a call for border security, a complex web of issues has emerged. This has led to increased inflation, higher immigration, food shortages, and an economic downturn, sparking unrest in the European Union and fulfilling this prophecy.

## Biblical Principles Related to this Word

In some respects, Jesus began his life in the middle of a housing crisis—there was no room in any of the inns or homes in Bethlehem for Mary and Joseph, so he was born into this world in a stable. Even in his later life, he lived as a nomad, spending the night in the homes of friends or sleeping outdoors under the stars. This is why he told his disciples, **"Foxes have holes and birds of the air *have* nests, but the Son of Man has nowhere to lay *His* head."—Luke 9:58**

*Pray that those suffering from homelessness will feel the nearness of Christ and that governments will have the wisdom to navigate these challenges well.*

There are global problems growing, but also a global move of God is on the horizon: the major systemic issues of immigration, weak borders, inflation, and economic trouble that are outlined in this prophetic word mirror the warnings that have been given to the United States in other prophetic messages in this book. This suggests that many of these issues are actually *global issues.* While it might be discouraging to see such monumental problems unfolding in the world, we should also recognize that the global turmoil we are being warned about will also lead to a global move of God and an unprecedented harvest of souls.

*Ask God to move in remarkable new ways in European nations.*

## 25

"I saw one European nation—I believe Germany— caught in a financial scandal involving Chinese bribery and cheating through banks and involving Hong Kong, which will be another example of China's tentacles."

## FULFILLMENT: Early Indicators, But Not Yet Fulfilled

## What has already happened to fulfill this word?

A high-ranking executive of a Chinese solar panel company was arrested in Germany for white-collar crimes, related to past EU trade measures against Chinese solar producers, dating back to 2015-2017 (Radowitz, 2023).

## What has not yet happened?

There are still many cases of Chinese corruption waiting to be exposed in various regions of the world, and particularly in Germany. This is far more likely to be revealed after an economic recession, which most indicators suggest will happen soon.

# Biblical Principles Related to this Word

The kinds of scandals that this prophecy warns about are rooted in deception because the word warns of Chinese agents using deception and bribery to compromise Germany's physical safety and economic stability.   Jesus warned about those who appear to have noble intent but actually have destructive purpose when He said:

**"Beware of false prophets, who come to you in sheep's clothing, but inwardly they are ravenous wolves" (Matthew 7:15).**

Likewise, scripture warns that "the love of money is the root of all kinds of evil.  Bribery can only happen in cases when greed has a firm root in both the briber and the one being bribed.  We can see clearly in Judas' life how the love of money corrupted his heart:

**"Then Judas, His betrayer, seeing that He had been condemned, was remorseful and brought back the thirty pieces of silver to the chief priests and elders, saying, 'I have sinned by betraying innocent blood'" (Matthew 27:3-4).**

## Prayer Strategies

- *Pray that leaders in Germany and Hong Kong will have the spiritual discernment to see through the false fronts that Chinese operatives may present.*

- *Pray for the exposure of Chinese-German bribery schemes and for the unfolding of God's greater purpose for both China and Germany.*

- *Pray that offers of bribery would be firmly rejected when offered to German officials.*

## 26

"I saw the beginnings of a new French Revolution. Last year I shared about Emmanuel Macron, not that he is the antichrist, but he will have a choice to make. A significant health crisis will weaken him and his power for a time, then he will reemerge with a heroic façade for overcoming the health crisis. Paris will become a hotbed of unrest and riots. The French people will become weary of unsustainable illegal immigration.

## FULFILLMENT: Partly Fulfilled

## What has already happened to fulfill this word?

- Protests and strikes erupted in France due to President Macron's push to raise the pension age without parliamentary approval. Demonstrators expressed anger at the move, leading to unrest and clashes with riot police in March 2023 (Reuters, 2023).

- Protests erupted in France after police fatally shot a 17-year-old on July 2, 2023. Demonstrations continued for five nights, resulting in over 700 arrests (Associated Press, 2023).

- An anti-immigration sentiment rose in France due to the riots. Mainstream politicians, particularly from the right, began associating immigration with social problems, contributing to the sentiment's growth ( Ganley 2023).

- On October 12, 2023, France banned pro-Palestinian protests due to a surge in antisemitic incidents following the conflict between Israel and Hamas. Despite the ban, pro-Palestinian demonstrators in Paris defied it, leading to confrontations with the police (Charlton, 2023).

- France has endured a tumultuous year marked by various sources of unrest. Amidst these challenges, the surge in anti-immigration sentiment has provided a political advantage to right-wing leaders.

## What has not yet happened?

Emmanuel Macron has not yet experienced a major health crisis according to the prophecy.

## Key Scriptures to Read and Pray Through

A revolution against tyranny that is driven by Biblical values can lead to a time of sustained national awakening and reformation. However, a revolution of anger and discontentment can also be a source of great instability and destruction. Therefore, it is important for us to pray that this will be the *right kind* of revolution. Scripture tells us:

**"Where *there is* no revelation, the people cast off restraint; but happy *is* he who keeps the law" (Proverbs 29:18).**

*Ask the Lord to give revelation to the French people so that they will cast off the restraints of the enemy.*

*Ask for a God-inspired revolution to bring reformation to France, similar to the spiritual awakening that happened in Eastern Europe and Russia around the time of the Iron Curtain's collapse (and the Berlin Wall's destruction) in 1989.*

**27**

"Resistance will also be shown to Italy's newly elected prime minister, Giorgia Meloni. She ran a campaign theme of God, family, and country. A major drug bust scandal involving drug cartels and money laundering through Italian banks will be revealed. Somehow, the Vatican will be drawn into this through a low-level cleric in the Catholic Church. It will make international headlines, but it will also become a picture of an international drug ring that was caught through Italy's banking system."

## FULFILLMENT: Partly Fulfilled

## What has already happened to fulfill this word?

- An economist known as "G" defrauded the Bank of Italy and the European Economic and Social Committee of hundreds of thousands of euros through a fraudulent scheme involving expense claims and misuse of his office. He was ordered to repay the money and sentenced to prison. However, G's whereabouts are unknown (Munster, 2023).

- Italian prosecutors seek to indict the Bank of China's Milan branch and almost 300 individuals for a €4.5 billion money-laundering scheme involving illicit funds transferred to China from Italy (BBC News, 2023).

- Opposition to Giorgia Meloni's leadership in Italy centers on concerns about her immigration policies, economic and environmental performance, and ties to far-right allies. Critics fear the resurgence of extreme nationalism in her rhetoric (Giuffrida, 2023).

## What has not yet happened?

Corruption has come to light within Italy's banking system, however, there has been no involvement from the Catholic Church.

## Biblical Principles Related to this Word

While there remains a remnant of many sincere Catholics who trust in Christ for their salvation and have an authentic relationship with Him, there is also a deep and disturbing history of politicization, corruption, and even great evil perpetrated by Catholic leaders. We can point to many of the positive historical contributions of the Catholic Church in history, but also to great evils they inflicted on the world, such as the Spanish Inquisition, the persecution and execution of many sincere believers who questioned Catholic orthodoxy, and recurring anti-Semitism.

**Editorial Note:** The Biblical principles outlined for deception and bribery in prophecy #25 also apply to this prophecy.

## Prayer Strategies

• *Ask God to send fiery reformers into the Catholic Church just as He has done in the past.*

• *Ask the Lord to expose any corruption among Catholic Church leaders quickly so that it can be appropriately dealt with for the benefit of the sincere and Christ-centered Catholics among them.*

**28**

"I saw a sudden airstrike from Israel against Iran, and the target will be a nuclear development facility in Iran. Benjamin Netanyahu's leadership will strengthen Israel's resolve to defend themselves from the growing threat of the Iranian government."

**FULFILLMENT: Conditions are in place for fulfillment**

## What has happened to create the conditions for this event to happen?

- In March of 2023, former Undersecretary of Defense Colin Kahl informed lawmakers that Iran's nuclear program was advancing rapidly, potentially allowing them to produce nuclear bomb components in about 12 days (O'Neill, 2023).

- Israeli Prime Minister Netanyahu and officials held secret meetings to prepare for possible action against Iran's nuclear program. Netanyahu emphasized Israel's intent of preventing Iran from having a nuclear weapon (Aitken, 2023).

- Then in October, Hamas launched a surprise attack on Israel, causing the deadliest day in Israel's history with over 1,400 casualties, including 14 Americans. In response, Israel declared war on Hamas and imposed a "complete siege" of Gaza (Kurilla, 2023).

- Hezbollah also attacked Israeli military posts on the Lebanon border. Israel's IDF responded with drone strikes. Hezbollah's deputy chief expressed readiness to join the Israel-Hamas conflict (Norman, 2023).

- These premeditated attacks on Israel were supported by Iranian officials who approved the operation during a meeting in Beirut, as reported by The Wall Street Journal.

- Collaboration between Iranian officers and Hamas had been ongoing since August and Iran's supreme leader, Ayatollah Ali Khamenei, publicly supported the attacks (Jerusalem Post, 2023).

- The Israeli official, Joshua Zarka, affirmed that Iran is attempting to transport strategic weapons through Syria, indicating an expansion of the conflict. Israel reportedly launched an airstrike on Aleppo Airport in response.

- This development follows concerns that Iran played a role in planning Hamas rocket attacks on Israel and that the war could escalate further in the Middle East if Hezbollah becomes involved (India Today, 2023).

## What has not yet happened?

While Iran and Israel remain entangled in an ongoing regional conflict, a direct strike on an Iranian nuclear facility has not happened yet. Despite the escalating tensions in the Middle East, and several factors lining up for the occurrence of that event, it remains absent.

*Editor's Note: In the original recording and transcript of the 40 Prophecies on December 29, 2022, Chris shared that he saw the nuclear facility that Israel would hit would be the Bushehr Nuclear facility in Iran. This detail seemed important to document in this book because this event has not yet happened at the time of writing.*

*[See the following two pages for Biblical Principles and Passages]*

## Biblical Principles Related to this Word

God made a promise to Abraham in Genesis 12:3, saying, **"I will bless those who bless you, and I will curse him who curses you."** Since the Lord is the same yesterday, today, and forever, this promise and warning still hold true. Our individual and national destinies are tied to our posture toward God's people.

The majority of the Bible's authors were of Jewish descent, and even Jesus, in His flesh, was a Jewish man. This is why the Bible instructs us to pray for the Jewish people. Psalms 122:6 says, **"Pray for the peace of Jerusalem: 'May they prosper who love you.'"**

In the New Testament, Paul shared his heart for the people of Israel. In Romans 10:1, he says, **"my heart's desire and prayer to God for Israel is that they may be saved."** He also declared in Romans 11:26 that all Israel will be saved. Therefore, we are encouraged to continue praying for Israel, as God has not finished His work with His people. He will lead them to a saving knowledge of the Lord Jesus Christ, and we pray for this fulfillment to come to pass.

## Model Prayer

*Father, remember your promises to Abraham, Isaac and Israel. Be faithful to them. Shower Your blessings upon the people of Israel, and may their eyes be opened to recognize Jesus as the Messiah. Pour out your Spirit upon the land of Israel and bring revival to the whole nation. Amen.*

# Bible Passage to Read and Pray Through:
## *The Restoration of Israel in Amos 9*

11 "On that day I will raise up
The tabernacle of David, which has fallen down,
And repair its damages;
I will raise up its ruins,
And rebuild it as in the days of old;

12 That they may possess the remnant of Edom,
And all the Gentiles who are called by My name,"
Says the Lord who does this thing.

13 "Behold, the days are coming," says the Lord,
"When the plowman shall overtake the reaper,
And the treader of grapes him who sows seed;
The mountains shall drip with sweet wine,
And all the hills shall flow *with it.*

14 I will bring back the captives of My people Israel;
They shall build the waste cities and inhabit *them;*
They shall plant vineyards and drink wine from them;
They shall also make gardens and eat fruit from them.

15 I will plant them in their land,
And no longer shall they be pulled up
From the land I have given them,"
Says the Lord your God.

—Amos 9:11-15

**29**

"I saw a bizarre cosmic event in the heavens. The Bible says there will be signs in the heavens above. It could be a solar flare or comet breaking through the Earth's atmosphere. It won't bring major destruction, but it will affect technology worldwide, cause power outages, and make international headlines."

## FULFILLMENT: Partly Fulfilled

## What has already happened to fulfill this word?

- Two strong solar flares erupted from the Sun in February, 2023. These powerful bursts of energy pose risks to technology and were monitored by NASA's Solar Dynamics Observatory (Interrante, 2023).

- The solar flares led to a temporary radio blackout over South America. Solar flares of this magnitude can potentially impact communication systems, especially high-frequency radio signals, in the area facing the sun during the flare (Malik, 2023).

- The sun unleashed its seventh X-class solar flare of the year, signaling a significant increase in solar activity. This explosion led to a shortwave radio blackout over southeast Asia, Australia, and New Zealand due to ionization of the Earth's atmosphere. The surge in X-flares suggests that Solar Cycle 25 is rapidly intensifying (Space Weather, 2023).

## What has not yet happened?

This year has witnessed sporadic solar flares affecting radio signals in certain regions. However, we have not encountered widespread global disruptions in power and technology. Scientists predict that such a scenario may take place next year as we approach the peak of this solar cycle.

## Biblical Principles Related to this Word

In Luke 21:25, Jesus prophesies the appearance of signs in the heavens, heralding His second coming to Earth. Throughout history, the heavens have declared the works of God, announcing His splendor (Psalms 19:1). This event is prophesied to impact the earth in some significant ways, but it will also won't bring serve as a clear sign of hope, pointing to the imminent arrival of the Lord of the stars and the Creator of the heavens.

As stated in Romans 8:19, **"all of creation groans for the revealing of the sons of God."** While hurricanes and fires plague the Earth, the heavens join in this chorus of longing — "Come, Lord Jesus!" Let us join both heaven and Earth in this sacred prayer.

## Model Prayer

*Lord Jesus, come to us. Grant us discernment to recognize the signs of Your return. Help us wait with patience and endurance as You are at the door. Manifest your presence and kingdom in this world. We unite our voice to the signs in heaven above and the groaning on earth below to pray, "Come Lord Jesus!"*

## 30

"The Russian-Ukraine situation will lead to Vladimir Putin using something like a dirty bomb—not a nuclear bomb."

## FULFILLMENT: Partly Fulfilled, Early Indications

## What has already happened to fulfill this word?

- Vladimir Putin confirmed the deployment of tactical nuclear weapons in Belarus, stating they'd be used only if Russia faced a threat (BBC, 2023).

- In later developments, Senior Russian official Dmitry Medvedev warned that Russia might use nuclear weapons if Ukraine takes Russian territory (Pennington, 2023).

- Russian President Putin reported strengthened Russian positions in Ukraine due to the failure of Ukraine's counteroffensive (Reuters, 2023).

## What has not yet happened?

While Putin has dramatically escalated his rhetoric regarding Russia's nuclear arsenal, no evidence suggests the use of a dirty bomb in Ukraine so far.

## Biblical Principles Related to this Word

God has the power to halt a nuclear bomb mid-air, as effortlessly as swatting a fly. It's essential to understand that while God allows wars to occur, He is not the one who initiates them. As James 4:1-2 emphasizes, conflicts originate within individuals due to unfulfilled sinful desires. However, Psalm 46:9 provides hope, declaring, **"He makes wars to cease to the end of the earth; He breaks the bow and cuts the spear in two; He burns the chariots with fire."** We can turn to God in prayer, seeking His intervention to end conflicts and bring about peace.

## Key Scriptures to Read and Pray Through

**"What is the source of quarrels and conflicts among you? Is not the source your pleasures that wage war in your members? You lust and do not have;** *so* **you commit murder. You are envious and cannot obtain;** *so* **you fight and quarrel. You do not have because you do not ask."—James 4:1-2 NASB1995**

**"He makes wars to cease to the end of the earth; He breaks the bow and cuts the spear in two; He burns the chariots with fire."—Psalms 46:9 NASB1995**

## Model Prayer

*God, we lift up the people caught in the midst of this conflict between nations. Grant them comfort, assistance, provision, and solace during these challenging times. We ask You to bring an end to this war, fulfilling Your purpose in both Russia and Ukraine.*

## 31

"The food shortages in 2023 will happen for several reasons: harvest issues, strange weather patterns and phenomena, and bizarre sickness in cattle and animals. This will also lead to more mass illegal immigration."

## FULFILLMENT: Fulfilled

## What has already happened to fulfill this word?

- Southern Europe faced a harsh winter drought, causing water use restrictions in France and Italy. Spain faced food shortage issues due to irreversible damage to over 3.5 million hectares of cereal crops like wheat and barley. Insufficient rainfall and rising temperatures are also contributing factors (Hill, 2023).

- Extreme weather, including snow, rain, and floods, has disrupted crop production in the U.S. Delayed plantings and bee disruptions are expected to lead to smaller selections, reduced supplies, and higher prices for fruits, nuts, and vegetables. Almonds, a significant crop, may see reduced yields due to a lack of bee pollination (Lee, 2023).

- Highly pathogenic bird flu reappeared in U.S. commercial poultry flocks in October, affecting turkey farms in South Dakota and Utah. It's the first such occurrence since April, raising concerns for the poultry industry and necessitating culling and biosecurity measures (Karnowski, 2023).

- A convergence of harvest challenges, unusual weather patterns, and cattle illnesses has precipitated food shortages and supply disruptions.

## Biblical Principles Related to this Word

- In Exodus 16, the Lord provided manna to sustain the people of Israel during their desert journey. In today's world, facing unparalleled financial challenges, it's essential to remember that the same God who feeds for the birds and dresses the flowers is our Father (See Matthew 6:25-34). It's wise to entrust all our burdens to Him, because He watches over us with care (See 1 Peter 5:7). God finds ways of providing for His people whenever they need it. He remains an ever-present Help for those who call upon His name.

- God blesses us to become a blessing, just as he said to Abraham in Genesis 12:2. His provision for us becomes the way He encounters others in their need as blessings flow through us to those who surround us. We can become a river of thanksgiving in His presence as we give thanks and share blessings with others.

## Model Prayer

*Father, we place our trust in you for our sustenance and livelihood. In this time of shaking, as the world goes through a period of uncertainty, we believe that we will see your glory. Open the heavens to provide for our families and show us how to be a blessing to others in a time of economic crisis and financial instability.*

## 32

"King Charles III will have his coronation in May 2023. Every British coronation for the last 1,000 years has included the "Stone of Scone" or "Stone of Destiny" set under the monarch's chair during coronation. This stone is believed to be one of the stones upon which Jacob laid his head when he had his dream. There will a bizarre mystery or uncertainty surrounding this stone at the time of Charles' coronation."

**FULFILLMENT: Fulfilled, but More Mysteries to Come**

## What has already happened to fulfill this word?

- The Stone of Destiny, also known as the Stone of Scone, has a long and contentious history. It was originally used for the coronation of Scottish kings at Scone Palace and had origins dating back to at least 1249. In 1296, it was seized by King Edward I of England, who incorporated it into the coronation throne at Westminster Abbey.
- In 1950, a group of students, including Ian Hamilton, successfully "repatriated" the stone, taking it from under the English throne and smuggling it to Scotland. The stone was later repaired and used for Queen Elizabeth's coronation in 1953. In 1996, it was officially returned to Scotland under certain conditions.
- The controversy lies in differing opinions about the stone's significance and where it should be used for coronations. Some argue for its return to Scotland, emphasizing its historical connection to Scottish monarchy, while others accept its role in English coronations as part of a symbol of unity and friendship (Goodyear, 2023).

- However, Alba Party leader and former Scottish First Minister Alex Salmond suggested that the stone held in Edinburgh Castle may not be the real one. Some believe the true Stone of Destiny is hidden, while others question its origin (Borland, 2023).
- The controversy enveloping the Stone of Destiny leading up to King Charles' coronation dominated headlines, casting a veil of doubt over the stone's provenance. This fulfills the prophecy shared above.

## Biblical Principles Related to this Word

- If the Stone of Scone legend is to be believed, it is worth noting that Jacob's stone may be lying beneath the highest seat of authority in the United Kingdom. According to the legend, this very stone was where Jacob had his dream, where he saw the heavens open. In this vision, he witnessed angels ascending and descending and even saw God, along with promises concerning his destiny (See Genesis 28).

- If we apply the pattern of Genesis 28 to the United Kingdom, we can discern a divine calling upon the U.K. to govern under an open heaven, implementing heavenly plans and policies that advance the Kingdom of God on Earth, just as we have seen in the long history of trans-Atlantic revivalism including Methodism, the Welsh Revival, and more. With this interpretation, the U.K. is tasked with showcasing the glory of a Gentile nation fully grafted into God's promises to Abraham.

## Prayer Strategies

*Father, we ask that You bring forth the destiny of the United Kingdom. Just as the heavens opened to Jacob, we ask that You open the heavens to the leadership of this nation. May they stand as a symbol of a redeemed Gentile nation, provoking Israel to jealousy. Amen.*

**33**

"Prince Andrew, King Charles' brother, will fall into a deep depression because of this, and legal troubles will arise because his mother is no longer there to protect him. A mental health crisis will make him suicidal. Pray for him. I saw him in a plea of desperation."

## FULFILLMENT: Partly Fulfilled

## What has already happened to fulfill this word?

- Prince Andrew met with King Charles, who informed him that he would never return to royal duties. This revelation left the Duke of York "completely lost and very depressed." He had hoped for a chance at rehabilitation (Eldridge, 2023).

- In the A&E documentary "Secrets of Prince Andrew," the deep connection between Prince Andrew and Jeffrey Epstein is revealed. Epstein had intimate knowledge of Andrew's life, and they were frequently seen together. Accusers like Lisa Phillips and Virginia Roberts Giuffre shared disturbing experiences. The documentary highlights Epstein's manipulative influence on Andrew (Ibrahim, 2023).

## What has not happened?

While Prince Andrew experienced profound disillusionment following his removal from royal duties, no reports have emerged suggesting suicidal thoughts.

# Key Scriptures to Read and Pray Through

> "He heals the brokenhearted and
> binds up their wounds."
> —Psalm 147:3

## Biblical Principles Related to this Word

- At the personal level, God exposes and reveals sin in individuals through the Holy Spirit's conviction so that they can respond with heartfelt repentance.
- The Pharisees condemned sinners for their sins, but they condemned Christ for showing mercy and grace. We want to have the opposite spirit—praying for heartfelt repentance and mercy for those who are struggling with the weight of sin and depression.
- It's vital to remember that before his conversion, Paul was a ruthless murderer, targeting not just anyone but specifically the followers of Jesus. In 1 Timothy 1:15, he acknowledges, **"Here is a trustworthy saying that deserves full acceptance: Christ Jesus came into the world to save sinners—of whom I am the worst."** This is why we pray even for those who've committed great wrongs because God's desire is for all to come to repentance and to know Christ intimately.

## Prayer Strategies

*Father, help Prince Andrew get out of this depression. Show him that You can turn a valley of desperation into a door of hope. Teach him your ways and bring him to deep repentance and a saving knowledge of Jesus Christ.*

## 34

"Regarding King Charles, I also saw a hot mic recording incident where the king made a tremendously embarrassing statement that will be used by other nations as propaganda. I saw on a headline the phrase, "loose lips sink ships." Royals will experience much humility, embarrassment, and contrition over this and will be apologetic as King Charles wrestles with his own humanity."

## FULFILLMENT: Not Yet Fulfilled

## What has not yet happened?

The royal family has experienced plenty of embarrassment over the years, but this specific "hot mic" incident has not yet happened.

## Key Scriptures to Read and Pray Through

**"Whoever guards his mouth and tongue keeps his soul from troubles."—Proverbs 21:23**

**"Even so the tongue is a little member and boasts great things. See how great a forest a little fire kindles!"—James 3:5**

## Biblical Principles Related to this Word

• God's way is to humble the proud and exalt the humble (James 4:6). In Luke 1:52, Mary proclaimed, **"He has brought down rulers from their thrones but has lifted up the humble."** Those in power are not exempt from God's humbling touch.

• As Matthew 12:37 reminds us, we are judged by the words we speak. The whispers of the "inner chamber" will be declared out loud, so we must be cautious in our speech, to honor the Lord with our words  (Luke 12:3).

• Words hold not only the power of condemnation but also of blessing and edification. Proverbs 18:21 asserts, **"Death and life are in the power of the tongue, And those who love it and indulge it will eat its fruit and bear the consequences of their words."** Speaking blessings and wisdom is a heart discipline that brings forth the sweetest fruits.

## Model Prayers

*Teach us to speak wisdom and to learn to be silent when there is nothing wise to say. Guide our words to be edifying for those who listen.*

*God, bring humility to the royal family beyond the embarrassment they may feel for this incident or others like. Allow them to see You are King of kings and Lord of lords. Teach us the art of speaking wisdom and the virtue of silence.*

## 35

"I have also seen in a vision more than once, and I do not wish this on anyone, but Prince Harry and Meghan will not stay together. When Meghan Markle pulls away from Prince Harry, he will see he was "played a fool" and will be repentant and contrite towards his family and heritage."

## FULFILLMENT: Partly Fulfilled

## What has already happened to fulfill this word?

- Prince Harry and Meghan Markle are dismissing rumors of a marital rift. Despite occasional separations due to work projects, they remain a united couple (MARCA, 2023). However, Royal biographer Angela Levin suggests Meghan Markle is planning to separate from Prince Harry, leaving him isolated in the U.S. Levin believes Meghan's actions may negatively affect Harry's mental health and claims she aims to secure custody of their children (Roy, 2023).

- The Duke and Duchess of Sussex have responded to divorce rumors with a PR campaign, emphasizing their strong and playful relationship. They are working on film projects and philanthropic initiatives, countering negative publicity (Jones, 2023).

## What has not yet happened?

Despite numerous rumors surrounding Prince Harry and Meghan Markle's relationship, the couple remains united. While some experts and commentators claim there are significant rifts in their partnership, no official separation has been confirmed.

## Key Scriptures to Read and Pray Through

**"It was good for me to be afflicted so that
I might learn your decrees."—Psalms 119: 71**

## Biblical Principles Related to this Word

• At times, God permits afflictions to enter the lives of individuals as a means for them to come to know Him (Psalms 119:71). In Daniel chapter 4, King Nebuchadnezzar was afflicted with mental illness until he finally acknowledged that **"His [God's] dominion is an eternal dominion; his kingdom endures from generation to generation" (Daniel 4:34).**

• While we may grieve over this prophecy, similar to how Daniel lamented for King Nebuchadnezzar, it is our calling to earnestly pray for repentance to touch the heart of Prince Harry.

• Just as the Lord instructed the prophet Hosea to marry a prostitute and then taught him many lessons through this unique marriage, the Lord may have important lessons to teach Harry from the struggles of his troubled marriage with Meghan.

## Prayer Strategies

*Father, we ask you to instill repentance in the heart of Prince Harry. Allow him to come to know you deeply. May he emerge as a door of hope for the Royal Family of England. Give him the resilience to withstand trials and tribulations, and eventually, reveal to him a profound understanding of Your presence. And give us the same grace to see you in the tests we face. Amen.*

## 36

"We will continue to see more and more famous people suddenly die, and there will be a reason for this. It will be something in their bodies. A major well-known Hollywood star will unexpectedly die, and this will result in further investigations into the COVID vaccines."

## FULFILLMENT: Partly Fulfilled

## What has already happened to fulfill this word?

- Buffalo Bills safety Damar Hamlin suffered a cardiac arrest during a game against the Cincinnati Bengals after a tackle. He received CPR and was transferred to a hospital, listed in critical condition. This happened on January 2nd, only days after this prophecy was shared (Maaddi, 2023). Although he survived this incident, it made national news and sparked a wave of prayers for the player (MAADDI, 2023).
- Sudden cardiac arrest is the leading cause of death in young athletes. Estimates vary, but some reports suggest that about 1 in 50,000 to 1 in 80,000 young athletes die of sudden cardiac death annually (Liu, 2023).
- A recent poll found that about a third of adults believed in the idea that COVID-19 vaccines caused sudden deaths, and a similar number thought that ivermectin was an effective COVID-19 treatment (CHOI, 2023).
- In January of 2023, Fox News host Dan Bongino talked about COVID-19 vaccines, highlighting a growing sense of distrust among recipients, even Democrats. Influential figures like Elon Musk and Scott Adams have expressed regrets about vaccination, while theories circulate, linking vaccines to deaths. Social media has seen videos purporting vaccine side effects, and a resurgence in anti-vax content. Notably, an anti-vax street

protest took place in the U.K., featuring prominent anti-vaxxer Robert F. Kennedy Jr. (Klee, 2023).

## What has not yet happened?

A "major Hollywood star" has not yet passed away as a result of the COVID-19 vaccine.

## Biblical Principles Related to this Word

- In an attempt to consolidate his control over Israel, King Jeroboam erected golden calves in the cities of Bethel and Dan, diverting worship away from the prescribed temple in Jerusalem (See 1 Kings 12:26-30. His motivation was rooted in the fear of losing his grip on power, ensnaring the people into this unorthodox worship, and people simply did as they were told.

- Similarly, many individuals have received the COVID-19 vaccine under the pressure and fear instigated by our federal government. What was initially presented as a solution to a significant problem has, for some, transformed into a problem itself. As Jesus warned about the end times, **"Take care that you are not deceived" (Matthew 24:4)**. The church must exercise discernment during these challenging times.

## Prayer Strategies

*Father, we pray that You make us a discerning people in this hour of deception. Grant us the wisdom that we need to remain in Your will, and teach us to trust in Your steadfast love and protection. Amen.*

**37**

"China will continue down the road of internal revolution which I first prophesied on October 1, 2022. It will lead to the end of Xi Jinping's rule. Then, I saw perhaps in five to ten years, China will devolve into region states or sections, and democracy and a whole new way of life will come to China. When Xi Jinping's power comes to an end, know that judgment has come to the Chinese Communist Party and its power hold on China will finally be broken."

## FULFILLMENT: Partly Fulfilled

## What has already happened to fulfill this word?

- In November 2022, Chinese protesters engaged in the "Blank Paper" movement, the blank piece of paper serves as a representation of everything protesters wish they could say but cannot (Amnesty International, 2023).

- Despite hi-tech surveillance, protesters persist and clamor for the ousting of Xin Jinping, even being subject to disappearances (Yu, 2023).

- China's property market crisis, triggered by a government crackdown on developer borrowing, threatens the nation's economic growth. Investment in real estate dropped, with forecasts of a 1.5% annual decline until 2026, impacting consumer spending and wealth (He, 2023).

## What has not yet happened?

Despite China's economic collapse, Xi Jinping maintains his grip on power and remains focused on Taiwan, which is regarded as a coveted prize due to its advanced chip manufacturing capabilities.

## Biblical Principles Related to this Word

In Daniel 2, the Lord is revealed as One who is sovereign over the kingdoms of this earth. The rule of unjust, oppressive governments has an expiration date. Daniel writes, **"He changes times and seasons; he removes kings and sets up kings" (see Daniel 2:21).**

In the same chapter, a statue symbolizing the various earthly kingdoms and empires across different eras is described. However, a Rock is cut out and cast at the statue, shattering it to pieces, and this Rock transforms into a mountain that fills the entire earth. As stated in Daniel 2:44, **"the God of heaven will set up a kingdom that will never be destroyed, nor will it be left to another people. It will crush all those kingdoms and bring them to an end, but it will itself endure forever."** This passage reveals a profound truth: amidst the rise and fall of all earthly kingdoms, there is one kingdom destined to last forever–God's kingdom in Christ.

## Model Prayer

*Father, we thank You for being a just God who sees the oppression of unrighteous governments. We ask You to break the back of communist power in China. In its place, raise up righteous leaders who can carry this nation into the new beginning You've destined. Thank you for giving us a kingdom that will last forever in Jesus. Amen.*

## 38

"The same judgment [as #37] is coming on Vladimir Putin, though he has taken a stand against the LGBTQ agenda. In recent years, Putin lost his godly influencers, and a vacuum has been created in his life. In 2023 or shortly after, we will see the end of Vladimir Putin's rule in Russia. Fear and paranoia will overcome him, and his worst fears will be realized. Those in his inner circle will even turn against him."

## FULFILLMENT: Mostly Fulfilled

## What has already happened to fulfill this word?

- Putin allowed a coven of witches in the Russian Capital to perform a "Circle of Power" ceremony, led by proclaimed hereditary witch leader Alyona Polyn (The Moscow Times, 2019).

- Russian President Putin condemned a rebellion by pro-Kremlin mercenary group Wagner, led by Yevgeny Prigozhin, accusing them of an "armed revolt." Wagner had been fighting in Ukraine alongside the Russian army, further complicating the ongoing conflict (Maynes, 2023).

- A defected Russian security officer, Gleb Karakulov, provided insights into Vladimir Putin's lifestyle, including a secret train network, identical offices, and a strict quarantine due to the Russian president's extreme paranoia. Karakulov described Putin's "pathological fear for his life" (Roth, 2023).

## What has not yet happened?

Putin has suffered from deep fear and paranoia, accusing even members of his inner circle of treason and conspiracy. However, Putin is still leader of Russia as of October 2023.

## Biblical Principles Related to this Word

- The counsel received by highly influential leaders is paramount to their success. Solomon writes, **"Where no counsel is, the people fall: but in the multitude of counselors there is safety" (see Proverbs 11:14).** Consider the story of Rehoboam, Solomon's successor to the throne of Israel. The people came to him promising their service with the request that their load be lightened. He sought advice from two factions – the elderly advisors of his father and his youthful friends. He heeded the heavy-handed, oppressive advice of the latter. His response enraged the people, and Israel rebelled against the house of David from that day forward (2 Chronicles 10:19).

- The absence of Godly advice in Putin's circle has resulted in a departure from wisdom. Because of this, he will be removed from his place. Let's pray that God grants him the wisdom to return to a place of true relationship with the Lord and that a time of reformation begins soon in Russia.

## Model Prayer

*Father, we ask for the salvation of Vladimir Putin's soul. Have mercy upon him and draw him into the knowledge of Your Son. Grant the Russian people the great revival that You've promised through Your prophets. Amen.*

## 39

"Two new energy sources are emerging.
A new development and energy source will
emerge that will not be stopped by big energy."

**FULFILLMENT: Not Yet Fulfilled, Some Precursors**

## What has already happened to fulfill this word?

- U.S. scientists at the Lawrence Livermore National Laboratory achieved a net energy gain in a fusion reaction for the second time since December. In an experiment at the National Ignition Facility on July 30, they generated more energy from fusion than the laser energy used to drive it, marking a significant scientific breakthrough (Reuters, 2023).

- The Stella Terra, a solar-powered car developed by students at Eindhoven University, completed a 620-mile test drive in Morocco and the Sahara without recharging. It demonstrated off-road capabilities and efficient solar panel technology, exceeding expectations with a 97% efficient converter (Boffey, 2023).

## What has not yet happened?

The "two new emerging energy sources" may actually be something that goes far beyond the two breakthroughs listed above, so we rate this word as "not yet fulfilled."

## Biblical Principles Related to this Word

• Creative solutions to solve problems sometimes come as "downloads" from the Lord, such as when the Lord inspired Noah to build the ark, gave specific blueprints to Moses for building the tabernacle, or inspired Joseph to mobilize an entire nation to prepare for times of famine. In the same way, the Lord can grant creativity and revelation to engineers, scientists, and inventors to help solve the challenges of modern times.

• While David started as a humble shepherd, God chose him for a divine purpose, empowering him to conquer giants. Similarly, as new energy sources emerge, they face challenges from established giants in the energy industry. But just as David fulfilled his purpose, we will witness these emerging energy sources fulfilling what God intended to do with them.

## Key Scriptures to Read and Pray Through

**"As for these four young men, God gave them knowledge and skill in all literature and wisdom; and Daniel had understanding in all visions and dreams."**
**—Daniel 1:17**

## Model Prayer

*Father, we ask that you bring forth righteous reform within our energy industry. May the pioneers of technology have prophetic creativity and share in the desires of your heart just as David did. May your purpose be fulfilled completely within the energy sector.*

*If big energy companies are opposing anything that you desire to give to your people, then let them fall just as Goliath did.*

117

## 40

"Senator Ted Cruz will be faced with a critical decision and a health issue which will influence the direction of his life. Please pray against this health crisis."

## FULFILLMENT: Not Fulfilled

## What has not yet happened?

- This word about Ted Cruz being faced with a "a health crisis" has not yet come to pass and we are praying that it will not come to pass at any point in the future.

- The word about Ted Cruz facing a "critical decision" is likely related to the health crisis that was prophesied. However, it is also certain that he faces many important decisions on a regular basis because of his role as a U.S. Senator, an outspoken conservative voice, and a defender of Judeo-Christian values. For this reason, let's remember him in prayer and ask the Lord to give him a long, healthy life and the "spirit of Wisdom and Revelation" (Ephesians 1:17).

## Key Scripture

"Confess *your* trespasses to one another, and pray for one another, that you may be healed. The effective, fervent prayer of a righteous man avails much."—James 5:16

## Biblical Principles Related to this Word

- Since Chris was led to ask the congregation to "pray against this health crisis," then this illness is likely rooted in spiritual opposition to his generally righteous contributions to our nation.

- A good strategy when dealing with demonic assignments is to use the authority that Christ delegated to us to "bind" the enemy and "loose" the power of Christ in a person's life (Matthew 18:18).

- Both Namaan and Hezekiah are high-level leaders who faced significant health crises in their day. Through the spoken word of the Lord's prophets, they were healed. Isaiah prophesied that fifteen years would be added to Hezekiah's life, and they were. Elisha counseled Namaan to dip in the Jordan River seven times in order to be healed, and he was (2 Kings 5). However, in both cases, there was a response required of the leader. Namaan had to humble himself and obey the word of the Lord —and Hezekiah wept in prayer before his request was granted (2 Kings 20).

## Prayer Strategies

- One effective way to pray for our leaders is with simple prayers of blessing, such as, *"I bless _____ with long life, healing, wisdom, and revelation in Jesus' name."*

- As priests in God's eternal kingdom, we have the unique authority to bless others, including our leaders and our blessings have real power to change peoples' lives and reset their course (1 Peter 2:9). Take time to bless the leaders that touch your life regularly, local leaders, and national leaders.

# APPENDIX 1:
# Warning Dreams of Terrorism in America

*"Be sober, be vigilant;
because your adversary the devil
walks about like a roaring lion,
seeking whom he may devour."*
—*1 Peter 5:8*

**INTRODUCTORY TEACHING**

# A Watchman's Responsibility

by Michael Fickess
*MorningStar University director and*
*MorningStar Journal News director*

**"But if the watchman sees the sword coming and does not blow the trumpet, and the people are not warned, and the sword comes and takes *any* person from among them, he is taken away in his iniquity; but his blood I will require at the watchman's hand" (Ezekiel 33:6).**

As a prophetic watchman, Ezekiel was warned about "a sword coming upon the land" and was sternly admonished by the Lord to warn the people so they could take action. The Lord made it clear to Ezekiel that if he failed to warn the people of the violence that was coming, then the prophet himself would be responsible for the bloodshed that happened (see Ezekiel 33:1-6). Likewise, as a prophetic ministry with global impact, our MorningStar leaders are compelled to share the warning words that have been entrusted to us so that decisive action can be taken to prevent the violence the enemy has planned for us, both by mobilizing prayer and by responding with real-world security interventions.

In Ezekiel's case, the people of Israel suffered all the violence he warned about because they did not believe his words or respond with the kind of prayer, repentance, and decisive action that would have prevented foreign invasion. Yet, there remains a bright glimmer of hope in this chapter for the Lord also told Ezekiel, **"he who takes warning will save his life"** (Ezekiel **33:5).** While the following warning dreams may be terrifying enough to bring some to despair, we are sharing them for a much more redemptive purpose. We believe that prophetic warnings of coming disaster can at many times be averted through prayer, repentance, and decisive action at both the local and the national level.

Scripture tells us: **"A prudent man foresees the difficulties ahead and prepares for them; the simpleton goes blindly on and suffers the consequences" (Proverbs 22:3 TLB).** In ancient times, the watchman of a city did not operate in isolation. He coordinated with other watchmen and gatekeepers so that when he sounded the alarm, the gates could quickly be closed to the enemy's advance. Likewise, the warnings in this chapter will only be effective if people take them seriously and respond quickly.

On the individual level, all of us can engage in daily intercession for the nation and cover our families and communities in prayer. We can also take steps to become more aware of our surroundings and strengthen our defenses at home, at work, and in our houses of worship. However, the bulk of our efforts are best spent in sustained and unified prayer for our nation. Our hope is that these warnings will reverberate not only throughout the Body of Christ, but also through the intelligence and security organizations who are have the sacred trust of defending our nation from both foreign and domestic attacks. The threats mentioned in this book can be averted or reduced if only we take these warnings seriously and prepare for them now.

**2023 PROPHETIC WARNING DREAM**

# "Jihadist Terror Cells on American Soil"

### by Chris Reed
*President, MorningStar Ministries*

*Adapted from the "MSJN Special Alert: Israel's War on Terrorism," which was broadcast on October 12, 2023. Significantly, this dream came to Chris a few days prior, on the same night that Israel was attacked by Hamas.*

On the night of Saturday, October 8, 2023, I had a dream in which I saw a map of the United States. When I saw the American southern border, I saw thousands of trained terrorists from Middle Eastern countries peppered among the six million-plus illegal immigrants who have crossed the border since President Biden took office.

The dream included a strange and unique scenario: I was given a cell phone or some type of communication device. It was somehow capable of reading encrypted communications that explained coordinated terrorist plots to hijack the U.S.

government and ultimately bring destruction to America. I remember somehow being able to read the words, *"So goes Israel, so goes America."*

The comparison between the October 8, 2023 terrorist attack on Israel and the risks that America now faces is clear. Just as the attack on Israel came through its southern border and was a breach of both security and intelligence, the same thing happened in the warning dream I was given about terrorists crossing the U.S. southern border—they were able to enter covertly because of failures in American intelligence and security.

In the dream, the terrorists were trained in the Middle East and took advantage of the open U.S. southern border in the time frame since the American withdrawal from Afghanistan. Next, I saw a Jihadist resurgence as a result of the vacuum left by the American withdrawal from Afghanistan. I read which nations the terrorists came from, and I remembered seeing many were from the "stan" nations —such as Afghanistan, Pakistan, Uzbekistan, etc. However, these were not the only foreign nationals warned of in the dream. They were also working in coordination with Mexican cartels to get into the United States and relocate themselves throughout the nation, as instructed by the "command" communication device they all had.

Next, I saw at least twelve dormant terrorist cells on the United States map. Initially, these terrorists were mostly taking shelter in sanctuary cities and were given contacts to connect with upon arrival in those local areas. They could establish themselves and work in the communities where they now lived. They were promised from "command" that their families would be financially rewarded and were even promised rewards in the afterlife for their compliance.

Among the twelve sleeper terrorist cells, I remembered a few geographic locations where they were most prevalent: Michigan,

Minnesota, Arizona, Texas, the Carolinas, and the Northeast, including the cities of Boston, New York, and Philadelphia.

Their plan was to control the actions of the U.S. government and dictate our foreign policy, defense posture, and response to world events by blackmailing the U.S. government with threats such as: "If you do not do this in a particular situation, we'll coordinate and detonate bombs simultaneously," or "if the government doesn't comply with our demands and wishes, we will respond with acts of terror."

The demands of these covert terrorists in America were made clear in the dream and included the following:

1. Don't use the U.S. military to attack or fight against the cause of Jihad.

2. Continue to send funds to Iran and other terrorist states to support them in the name of "foreign aid."

3. They had explicit pictures of U.S. politicians in every branch of government, which they threatened to use if the U.S. crossed any "red line."

Explosions were the last step, but before that, they would attack our infrastructure with blackouts and other technological disruptions as other means of controlling the U.S. government. They could also coordinate mass shootings, knife attacks, and the taking of hostages in various places in the U.S. for ransom.

Finally, I saw a detonation happen across the U.S. with smoke clouds, rubble, destruction, and disaster all over the map.

I woke up knowing that if prayer and action are taken now, we can stop this. However, just like this attack came from the southern border of Israel, the terrorists in the dream came through the U.S. southern border. We must take immediate action: we need to pray, watch, listen, and be alert with situational awareness and self-defense training, so as not to be perceived as "soft targets."

**2014 PROPHETIC WARNING DREAM**

# The Southern Border and the Gates of Hell

by Rick Joyner

*Founder, MorningStar Ministries*

*Excerpt from MorningStar Prophetic Bulletin, #88, October 1, 2014*

The recent breaches in the White House security are not only shocking, they are prophetic. It was just revealed that the man who recently jumped the White House fence did not just make it to the front door, but actually got inside the White House, and deep inside of it. He was tackled by an off-duty agent who "just happened to be passing by."

This breach into what is considered the most important house in America is a reflection of the breakdown of security for the whole nation. Those whose most basic responsibility is the defense of our country have not done their job. They have left us vulnerable, and our enemies are now pouring through our porous borders.

In the prosecution of a crime, you look for a motive, means, and opportunity. Those with the motive to kill Americans and destroy America now have the means and opportunity because of the failure of our government to secure our borders. It does not take a genius or a prophet to know our enemies are not going to let such an opportunity pass by, and our government is leaving the front door open to them, just like the front door of the White House was left open. We are more vulnerable to terrorist attacks now than we have ever been. We will soon pay a terrible price if this is not addressed with the greatest resolve. The most basic responsibility of the federal government is defense, and the most basic defense of a nation begins with securing its borders. Our government leaders are presently guilty of the most basic dereliction of duty or treason. It must be one or the other.

## The Dream

On the night of September 17, I had a prophetic dream. It was about a "gate of hell" that has been opened into the United States. "Gates of hell" are the doors that hell uses to gain access. We have one of the biggest of these open into our country right now—our southern border.

This does not mean that everyone illegally crossing our borders is a terrorist or has evil intent. It is likely that just a small fraction want to do us harm, but this is enough to wreak havoc on the entire country and soon. In the dream, I was shown the unimaginable consequences we will suffer if our borders are not secured very soon.

The dream began with a gang that crossed our border to attack a ranch in Texas. They herded together everyone on the ranch, about twenty in all, including family and workers. There

130

were several children. Then with diabolical cruelty, they raped and tortured them. Then they killed them all in the most cruel, diabolical way imaginable. What they did to the children was the worst of all. Then they left with great excitement and celebration to attack another ranch. This was done in broad daylight. They did not seem at all concerned that they might be caught.

Then it was as if I was high over the land. I saw waves of gangs. Some appeared to be military units, sweeping across the southwestern United States. It was like a great plague as they were pillaging, plundering, raping, and murdering. It was an invasion that threatened more Americans than any previous war in our history. I was surprised I did not see any U.S. military response to this invasion.

Even though the invaders were pouring into every southwestern state, there was a special focus on Texas. They seemed to have a special hatred of Texas and Texans. After Texans, it seemed their rage was directed toward Hispanics. This was hard to understand since most of the invaders were Hispanics, but this is what I saw. We know that the insanity that came upon Rwanda turned Rwandans against Rwandans for even slightly perceived differences. In this kind of evil rage, reason can be very twisted. What I witnessed was a raging and insane brutality like the earth may have never faced before.

ISIS and other terrorist groups were part of this horde, but this was not an ISIS-led operation. In fact, the Islamic terrorists who were involved were shocked themselves by the level of diabolical evil they witnessed in these gangs. I knew that what I was seeing was the evil spirit of modern terrorism mixed with ancient spirits of a deep and powerful witchcraft from some of the South and Central American countries. The main evil spirit that was driving this was ancient, possibly rooted in old civilizations like the Mayans. When this mixed with the evil of terrorism, it became a concoction of evil like the world has never seen.

As this onslaught unfolded in the Southwest, I then saw an outrage sweep across America. This rage was not directed at the invaders as much as it was directed at our federal government because it had failed to protect us. This outrage grew to the point of being nearly as diabolical as what I had seen in the invasion across our border. Many Americans wanted to do to our government leaders what was being done to Americans in the border states. Every foolish action or policy our federal government had in regard to border security, such as the Fast and Furious program, was being brought up again to accuse our government. The rage grew with each one recited. I then saw federal employees fleeing some states as if they were fleeing for their lives. There was a seeming universal rejection of the federal government's authority by the states.

Then militia groups began popping up like mushrooms in a forest all across America. These were not racist or extremist militias, but rather ordinary citizens who were resolved to protect their families and neighbors. However, because of the rage in America, I felt these groups were vulnerable to being co-opted by extremist groups. Even so, in prophetic dreams and visions sometimes you just know things that you do not see. I knew that these militia groups would eventually stop the gangs that had come across our borders. This was because of the help they received from many veterans of Iraq and Afghanistan who knew how to fight this type of warfare.

At this time, county sheriffs became like the glue that held America together and kept it from a meltdown into anarchy. They took a leading role in security and defense against the attacks— not just those coming across the southwestern border, but those that seemed to be happening all over the nation.

I woke up with a most startling supernatural manifestation in my room that I still do not understand. I know it is significant, and I will share it when I am given understanding.

## This Can Be Prevented

Many prophetic warnings are given so that we understand the schemes of the devil in order to foil them. What I saw in this dream will happen if quick, decisive action is not taken to secure our southern border.

Days before I had this dream, I was told that America is in a Valley of Decision between now and the end of this year. When I asked what decisions we had to make, I did not get an immediate answer. However, when I had this dream, I knew it was the answer. If our government does not secure our borders very quickly, every American will be living in a constant danger from terrorist attacks. We will see the kind of wholesale invasion along our southwestern border that I saw in the dream.

Prophetic timetables do not revolve around U.S. elections, but the upcoming elections are right in the middle of this time of decision that we have been given. As I have been warning since the 2000 elections, every election from then on would be more important than the previous ones for the future of our country, including midterm elections. This has proven true. If we don't vote, then we are voting for evil, because evil will fill every vacuum that the righteous allows. We must pray that securing our borders becomes a major issue in the elections and that those who see and understand it are elected.

There are other fateful decisions that will be made that will determine whether or not we suffer the onslaught that I saw in the dream. We will know by the end of the year if the right ones were made. If not, then we will know it is time to prepare the homeland for the war that is coming. When serious preparation begins, a spirit of mockery will be released by the enemy to thwart it and keep us vulnerable.

# The Christian Response

This is the most alarming dream I have ever had. I admit to being shaken for days by it. I don't think I had any fear for myself or my family who I have entrusted into the hands of the Lord. I have seen a lot of evil, but I have not seen anything like this. It shook me deeply. Even so, as Christians we must not walk by fear but by faith. We must wake up, but we must also resolve that we will not take action out of fear. Fear is not a fruit of the Holy Spirit. If we are led by fear, we are not led by the Holy Spirit.

When the Lord told of all the things that would come upon the world at the end of the age, He told His people to do two things: first to stand up and then look up. It is time for the righteous to stand up. The scariest thing in all of Scripture is the lake of fire. We are told in Revelation 21:8 that the first group thrown into the lake of fire will be the cowards. There is no place for cowardice in Christianity. It is time for Christians to stand up and demonstrate the faith we have in the One who is above all rule and authority and dominion. As Paul wrote in Galatians 1:10, if he still feared men, he would not be a bondservant of Christ. No true servant of the Lord can be ruled by the fear of man, but rather by the true and holy fear of the Lord.

It is time for the righteous to look up and see that the Lord is on His throne. He is not wringing His hands in worry, and neither must we. He is preparing for His kingdom to come and so must we.

We are commanded to pray for our leaders. We are not told to just pray for the ones we like or agree with, but the ones we have. We must pray for our present leaders, that they will wake up and be given wise counsel so that this gate of hell into our country is shut. That is the best of all scenarios.

By the end of this year, we will know if the invasion I saw in the dream has been avoided or not. If not, it does not mean that the attack will come right then, but we will know it is inevitable. That is when we must begin to prepare for it. We will be given wisdom to do this. Until then we should pray earnestly that it is not necessary.

When I shared this dream on MorningStar Television, I was surprised by how fast it went viral. I was more surprised by how many had already foreseen this type of thing coming and were already preparing for it. I was especially encouraged to learn the number of sheriffs who are not only aware of these threats to our country but are preparing for them. It is obvious that God is preparing us in many ways.

Last year I was told that this year we would start to see the Lord as our Shepherd in a greater way than we have before. As terrible as this dream was, since having it I have become aware of just how much our Shepherd is watching over us and helping us be ready for things we may be completely ignorant of. This is wonderful to see, but let us also keep in mind as Psalm 23 makes clear, knowing Him as our Shepherd requires us to come to the table, even in the presence of our enemies and while going through the Valley of the Shadow of Death. Through all of this we will know, as we never have before, the Lord as our Shepherd and that He is able to keep us.

There is much more to discuss about natural, practical preparation for what is coming, but spiritual preparation is far more important. As Christians, we know that Satan cannot cast out Satan. The rage I saw coming upon Americans toward government leaders who had allowed this was diabolical too. Responding in rage is not the answer and will only multiply the access evil has in our country. Our non-Christian neighbors do not know this, and many will get caught up in this rage. Rage and revenge will try to fill America, yet Christians must stand up against this evil too.

When we begin to suffer the kinds of attacks I saw in this dream, it is understandable that the states would want to reject the federal government's authority over them. It is understandable that citizens will want to hold government officials accountable for what has been allowed. Righteousness and justice are the foundations of the Lord's throne, but His justice is never driven by rage.

What I saw coming upon the citizens and the states seemed to be leading to a breakup of the United States, not into just two nations but many. Our name is United States, and if we break up in this way, our major purpose will have been thwarted. This is the main scheme of the enemy in this attack. As Christians we must resolve not to let this happen. There may be a place for returning much more authority to the states and reducing the power of the federal government over the states to what was intended by the Constitution, but breaking up the country is only going to make everyone far more vulnerable. Christians will be the key factor that holds the country together or allows it to split apart.

One of the major purposes of the United States is to be light to the nations in confronting one of the ultimate evils of the human heart—racism. Racism is one of the ultimate evils because it is the result of the ultimate evils of fear and pride. We become racists because we fear those who are different from us, or we think we are better than others because of externals. We are warned, "God resists the proud, but gives grace to the humble" (see James 4:6 NKJV). The grace of God is more valuable than any earthly treasure. We should therefore resist pride in every way that we can. This begins with resisting thinking we are better than others because of the color of our skin.

The United States has had terrible racial problems in our history. We still have major problems, but we have confronted them and made remarkable progress overall, even if we continue to have occasional, serious setbacks. The U.S. is a nation that is made up of all nationalities, and that has been one of our greatest strengths. We need to build on this strength.

When the Lord was asked about the signs of the end of the age, one of the first things He said was, "Nation will rise against nation" (see Matthew 24:7). The Greek word translated "nation" in these verses is *ethnos* from which we derive the English word "ethnic." He wasn't talking about countries fighting each other, but that one of the biggest events at the end of the age would be ethnic conflicts. Possibly more than any other nation, America is now positioned to be a standard to the world of the power of ethnic groups living in peace and harmony with one another. It is the devil's intent to reduce America to a most deadly ethnic conflict. Christians, not the government, will determine which it will be.

It does not take a prophet to see that if what I saw in this dream unfolds, our Hispanic neighbors will be the most threatened. We are commanded to love our neighbors. The commandment does not specify their nationality, or even whether or not they are legal neighbors. If we love our neighbors, we will protect them from any threat, and as Christians we must resolve to do this. As Christians we must resolve now to stand up for and help any vulnerable people.

The truth is that Hispanic people are some of the easiest people in the world to love. Of all the ethnic groups America is made up of, Hispanics would rank at or very near the top of those who have been the greatest blessing to America. As we are told in I John 4:18, "There is no fear in love; but perfect love casts out fear...." If we are obeying God to love our neighbors, then we will not fear them regardless of any ethnic differences. If we love them, we will help protect them.

We must resolve now to grow every day in faith, not fear. We must resolve that we will grow in love and not fear. We must resolve to grow in the peace of God, not anger. Then the joy of the Lord will be our strength.

## Summary

"If you do not change your course, you will end up where you are headed." This dream represents where we are headed. The dream was so intense and powerful that I woke up feeling that this was imminent, but I was not given a specific timing in the dream for when this onslaught would come. The television show I did on this dream went viral, and sometimes exposing a scheme of the enemy to the light does at least cause him to pause, which can give us more time. I pray this is the case.

Even so, we do not have any time to waste. If the right decisions are not made by our government leaders by the end of this year to be decisive and resolute in defending our country by securing our borders, then we will need to start preparing for these things with decisiveness and resolve, but not in fear. The prepared prosper in all times.

Let us all make the right decision to vote in the upcoming elections. Because of ISIS, national defense has risen to the top of the issues, and it should be. We are vulnerable as a nation, just as security breaches to the White House should be a clear sign. The hedge of protection around our country is being removed by our leaders doing the things that we are warned will cause this to happen. Let us pray for our leaders to turn back to God or be replaced by those who will.

The only thing that will ultimately save our nation is another Great Awakening that turns the nation back to God. This onslaught across our southern border did not turn America back to God, but it turned Americans against one another. If this is not stopped, then it can still be lessened by wise leadership and wise preparation.

The most important preparation of all is for every Christian to truly elevate God's house above the White House, or any other house including our own. We must seek first His kingdom, which means that all of our major decisions should consider the purposes of God above any other purpose. His kingdom is built on a Rock that cannot be shaken. If we have built our houses on this Rock, we will not be shaken either.

*You shall not be afraid of the terror by night,*
*Nor of the arrow that flies by day,*

*Nor of the pestilence that walks in darkness,*
*Nor of the destruction that lays waste at noonday.*

*A thousand may fall at your side,*
*And ten thousand at your right hand;*
*But it shall not come near you.*

*Only with your eyes shall you look,*
*And see the reward of the wicked.*

*Because you have made the Lord, who is my refuge,*
*Even the Most High, your dwelling place,*

*No evil shall befall you,*
*Nor shall any plague come near your dwelling;*

*For He shall give His angels charge over you,*
*To keep you in all your ways.*

*—Psalm 91:5-11*

**TERROR THREAT DOCUMENTATION**

# Praying Through the Facts on the Ground

Our *MorningStar Journal News* team compiled the following list of "facts on the ground" in order to document the real-world threats and measurable trends that directly confirm the serious prophetic warnings given by Chris Reed and Rick Joyner. Our hope is that this additional level of confirmation will compel readers to pray with fervor and take steps to ensure the safety and security of their families, their workplaces, and their houses of worship.

While we have provided prayer strategies for the forty prophecies, the serious matter of an imminent terrorist threat is a call for more than intercession. Families and church leaders need to inquire of the Lord for themselves and engage in serious fasting and prayer to gain strategy from the Lord directly. Just as Gideon was given strategy to overcome the oppression of the Midianites and Elisha was given power to overcome the Arameans, we are confident that the same God of Israel will help you and your loved ones to hear clearly from heaven as we face this environment of increased threat.

# 1. Documented Threats from Unvetted Illegal Immigration

- In September, Border Patrol encountered 218,777 individuals at the U.S.-Mexico border, marking a record for the month and fiscal year 2023.
- This surge surpassed 2 million apprehensions for FY 2023, with the previous high in September 2022 at 207,597 encounters. Customs and Border Protection emphasized their commitment to combating human smuggling and criminal organizations.
- The Biden Administration announced that it would continue the construction of president Trump's border wall. This marks a significant shift of policy since Biden stopped the construction of the border wall as soon as he entered office (TAER, 2023).
- In a report, it is revealed that over 1.5 million illegal immigrants, termed as "gotaways," have entered the United States during the Biden administration. These individuals managed to evade capture, with an estimated 530,000 in fiscal year 2023, adding to the 600,000 from 2022 and 389,000 from 2021.
- This total is nearly four times the estimated 415,000 "gotaways" during the Trump administration's final three years (Hauf, 2023).
- Of the more than 5 million illegal alien encounters from January 20, 2021, through March 31, 2023, at least 2,464,424 illegal aliens had no confirmed departure from the United States as of March 31, 2023.
- Of the illegal aliens encountered in those 26 months, DHS released at least 2,148,738 illegal aliens into the United States.
- Of the at least 2.1 million aliens released into the United States since January 20, 2021, the Biden Administration has failed to remove, through immigration court removal proceedings, roughly 99.7 percent of those illegal aliens.
- These data contradict Secretary Mayorkas's statements that the southwest border is closed and that illegal aliens are "quickly" removed.10 Instead, with more than 99 percent of illegal aliens

staying inside the United States after being released by the Biden Administration, there is virtually no enforcement of our immigration laws (U.S. House of Representatives, 2023).

## 2. Documented Threats from Mexican Cartels, Drug Traffickers, and other Criminals

- Texas authorities have seized over 422 million deadly doses of fentanyl at the border since 2021, which would be enough Fentanyl to kill the entire U.S. population. Governor Greg Abbott has attributed this large seizure to President Biden's "open border policies." The fentanyl seizure is part of Texas' efforts to combat drug trafficking and enhance border security (Martinez, 2023).
- Mexican Cartels, including the Jalisco New Generation Cartel and Sinaloa Cartel, are the primary drivers of the fentanyl crisis in the United States, leading to a drug overdose epidemic.
- Operation Last Mile, a year-long investigation by the DEA's New Orleans Field Division, resulted in the seizure of over 147,000 fentanyl pills and 63 pounds of fentanyl powder, aimed at disrupting the last mile of the cartel-to-local distributor drug supply chain (Castor, 2023).
- In 2022, the US witnessed a staggering increase in fentanyl overdose deaths, totaling 73,654—more than double the count from 2019. In 2022, Fentanyl was the underlying cause of nearly 70% of drug overdose deaths.
- Fentanyl, an opioid 50 times stronger than heroin and 100 times stronger than morphine, poses a grave risk due to its potency. The surge in fentanyl-related fatalities is linked in part to the mixing of fentanyl with other drugs (USA Facts, 2023).
- Mexican cartels profit from effective and lucrative human smuggling operations at the southern border. Human smuggling operations' profits have surged, reaching $13 billion as of July 2022, up from $500 million in 2018. Cartel fees for migrants attempting to cross the border can range from $4,000 to $20,000.

- Cartels use the migrant surge to smuggle drugs into the U.S. CBP seized 15,000 pounds of fentanyl along the southern border in 2022, marking a 206% increase since 2020. Drug trafficking by migrants is one method to pay off their debts to cartels. Mexican cartels are essentially controlling the border, funneling both people and drugs across.
- Nearly 100 known or suspected terrorists were arrested at the southern border in the past year. Migrant encounters at the border increased dramatically, from 480,000 in 2020 to 2.3 million in the last year (Myers, 2023).

## 3. Documented Threats from Illegal Immigrants Originating from "—STAN" Countries

- The Biden administration detected and halted a human smuggling network attempting to bring people from Uzbekistan into the United States.
- At least one member of the smuggling network had links to a foreign terrorist group, believed to be the Islamic State.
- The U.S. worked with foreign governments to apprehend key members of the network and is actively shutting down the travel routes used by smugglers, while migrants associated with this network are being vetted and detained (SANTANA, 2023).
- Also, leaked Customs and Border Protection's data reveals the apprehension of "special interest aliens," individuals from countries of national security concern, attempting to cross the U.S. southern border illegally between October 2021 and October 2023.
- Over the past two years, over 70,000 migrants, including nationals from Afghanistan, Iran, and Syria, designated as 'special interest aliens,' were detained at the U.S. southern border
- Border Patrol agents express worries about vetting these individuals as their criminal histories are often unknown, given that their home countries do not share data with the U.S.,

posing challenges in ensuring the safety of the border and the country (Melugin, 2023).

- Lora Ries, director of the Border Security and Immigration Center at The Heritage Foundation, expressed concerns about the existence of "sleeper cells" in the U.S. She pointed to pro-Hamas protests in the U.S. as a public signal that such cells may be active. Ries emphasized that these cells don't need to enter via the border but are already present (Miller, 2023).

- Since President Biden took office, 268 encounters with individuals on the terrorist watchlist attempting to enter the U.S. illegally have been reported by the U.S. Border Patrol. In contrast, during President Trump's four years in office, only 14 such encounters were documented, indicating a significant increase under the current administration.

- The encounters in fiscal year 2021 numbered 16, rising to 98 in 2022, and 154 in 2023, highlighting the growing trend during President Biden's tenure (Matthews, 2023).

## 4. Notable Weaknesses and "Gaps in the Wall" with Local Law Enforcement

- Murder rates in major US cities have surged by over 10% in the past two years, with the most significant increases occurring in cities led by Democratic, left-wing mayors.

- A study by WalletHub compared the rise in murder rates between 2021 and 2023 in 45 of the country's most populous cities, revealing a faster increase in homicides in Democrat-led cities compared to Republican-led ones.

- The Covid-19 pandemic contributed to the initial rise in homicides, but scholars suggest that soft-on-crime policing and a decrease in proactive policing, partly due to social unrest, have exacerbated the issue.

- Progressive policies like defund the police and implementing no-cash bail are seen as major factors contributing to the rising national homicide rate (Donlevy, 2023).

- Major U.S. cities, once declared as sanctuary cities for illegal immigrants, are reconsidering their immigration policies due to the financial and social impacts of an influx of millions of illegal immigrants since President Biden took office.
- This growing trend of sanctuary cities reevaluating their stance may lead to a reexamination of federal immigration policies, as local leaders grapple with the consequences of their previous support for such policies. Law enforcement officials are concerned about the safety implications of sanctuary city policies, as they often lack access to the criminal histories of illegal immigrants with prior records, who may pose risks to public safety (Harper, 2023). A "sanctuary" city is where local and state law enforcement do not cooperate with federal immigration enforcement, creating a welcoming atmosphere for illegal immigrants.
- Chicago recently revealed a $538 million budget deficit, with a significant portion attributed to costs related to caring for new migrants arriving in the city. A substantial portion of the deficit is linked to special project costs associated with migrant care (Shaw, 2023).
- New York City Mayor Eric Adams has expressed concern about the growing number of migrants in his city, warning that it could destroy the city. Adams emphasized that he doesn't see an end to the crisis and has sought help from state and federal authorities to address the housing and care needs of asylum seekers. Adams estimates there are already 110,000 migrants in the city, with approximately 10,000 more arriving each month. A majority of New Yorkers agree that the migrant influx is a serious problem, according to a recent poll (Rahman, 2023).
- Texas Department of Public Safety data reveals that illegal immigrants have higher conviction rates for serious crimes, such as homicide and sexual assault, compared to the general population. Also, the relative crime rate of the illegal-immigrant population in Texas, as indicated by convictions, challenges the notion of lower crime rates among this group (Camarota, 2022).

146

# Partial Map of Terror Cells Apprehended in the United States (with group affiliation)

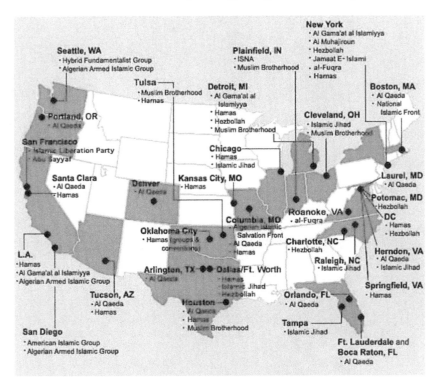

**Source:** The above map reflects research from Steven Emerson (author of *American Jihad, 2002)* and independent investigators and news agencies. Although this map does not reflect every apprehension and represents a smaller sampling, it does demonstrate the regional vulnerabilities that Chris Reed highlighted in his warning dream, "Terrorism on American Soil."

## APPENDIX 2:
# Prophetic Words for Israel, America, and the Nations

"THE $50 BILL DREAM"
*2022 Warning Dream by Chris Reed*
- 151 -

"THE WAR ON ISRAEL AND THE WICKED CITY"
*2018 Warning Dream by Rick Joyner*
- 157 -

THE SPIRITUAL RESURGENCE OF THE PRINCE OF PERSIA
(WITH ADDITIONAL PROPHECIES FOR OTHER NATIONS)
*By Chris Reed*
- 161 -

*"But I'm not bound and I never will be
to a wrinkled, crinkled, wadded dollar bill."*

**—Johnny Cash,**
*Lyric from "Wrinkled, Crinkled,
Wadded Dollar Bill"*

# The $50 Bill Dream

by Chris Reed, *President of MorningStar*
With Rick Joyner, *Founder of MorningStar*

*Chris Reed received the following dream on March 25, 2022. Rick Joyner adds some of his interpretation after each section in parentheses and italics. Although this dream has been available online since Spring of 2022, this is the first time it has appeared in traditional print for the readers' long-term benefit and stewardship.*

### The Dream

I saw an unknown man dressed in a black suit holding a fifty-dollar bill. He tore the fifty-dollar bill in three stages. In the first stage of the dream, he stood in front of me, took the fifty-dollar bill, and tore off a third of it. As he did, random people started bringing me national newspapers one after another. All I could read were the headlines.

*(RJ: Johnny Cash was known as the "Man in Black" and the fifty dollars is of course cash. Johnny Cash dressed in black also represents a*

151

*mourning for the moral and spiritual depravity growing in America. Chris felt the fifty-dollar bill represented the fifty states. Fifty is also the number of the Jubilee, and at the end of this dream is a restoration the Jubilee accomplishes.)*

The first headline read, **"The Dollar Drops Thirty Percent in Value: Mideast Oil Strikes Deal with China Instead of U.S."**

*(RJ: Between the U.S. dollar no longer being backed by anything but trust in the U.S. government and the recent ineptness of our governmental leaders on world economic issues, we see the beginning of a worldwide flight toward a more stable economic world leader. Looking to China for leadership is a shocking demonstration of how much faith and trust America has lost in just the past year. We need to prepare for a serious devaluing of the U.S. dollar.)*

Another headline read, **"The Perfect Storm: Inflation Reaches a New High."**

*(RJ: Inflation is one of the most devastating crises any nation can face. In the U.S. right now it is at a forty-year high and it is much higher than is being reported by our government. The devaluing of our dollar by 30% could mean another 30% jump in inflation. If we add up the disastrous economic policies implemented during COVID, the worsening supply chain crisis with no corrective governmental action, and the Biden "Green New Deal" energy policies, we are heading for an economic "Perfect Storm" that could shake our economy like never before. We should all take immediate action to prepare for this.)*

I was then handed another headline which read, **"Food Shortage Crisis as Wheat and Bread Imports are at Stalemate."**

*(RJ: During a recent visit to Poland, President Joe Biden finally admitted there will be food shortages. What we at MorningStar have*

been warning about for more than a decade is now upon us and will be more severe than our government is admitting. Ukraine is not only the "breadbasket of Europe" but also "of the world." The U.S. imports much of its wheat from Ukraine. Thus, the Russian invasion will have a major impact on world food supplies, including ours.)

Another headline was handed to me which read, **"Riots and Civil Unrest as Citizens Demand Entitlement Checks."**

*(RJ: Riots and civil unrest are inevitable because nearly half of Americans are now dependent on government programs and our government does not have the wisdom or resources to meet what will soon be upon us. Those who are not personally prepared and resourceful and are dependent on the government to take care of them will be desperate. They will riot and seek to plunder those who are prepared.)*

In the second stage of the dream, I again saw the man dressed in black holding the rest of the fifty-dollar bill, and this time he tore it in half. As he did, I felt an earthquake under my feet. A person walked up and handed me a headline which read, **"Israeli and Palestinian Two-State Solution Reached."**

*(RJ: The prophet Bob Jones warned us for years that when the U.S. tried to pressure Israel to give up more land for peace, the New Madrid Fault Line in the middle of the U.S. would literally tear our country in two by destroying all the bridges across the Mississippi River. This seems tied to the next headline Chris saw in his dream.)*

Another person handed me another headline which read, **"Major Earthquake Hits the Middle of the U.S."**

*(RJ: Bob saw and warned us for years that when the New Madrid Fault Line went it would destroy much of the heartland of America, even transforming its geography. This is the breadbasket of*

*our country, which could only exacerbate the problems of inflation and food shortages created by our government.)*

In the third stage of the dream, the man in black took the rest of the fifty-dollar bill and started tearing it into smaller pieces, one by one. A person walked up and handed me another headline which read, **"America in Pieces: More States Secede from the Nation in Rebellion to the Federal Government."**

*(RJ: The American people and many state government leaders know the policies of our federal government have led to the crises tearing our country apart. I too have had several prophetic dreams about the states and the people turning against the federal government and breaking up into smaller regional districts.)*

I was then handed another headline which read, **"U.S. Military Takes Charge as Uncertainty Looms over Federal Government."**

*(RJ: I was first shown in 1987 that the U.S. would go through a period of martial law. Since then, I have had many corroborating dreams or visions about this. The exhortation I received in 1987 was to start praying for this military leader to be committed to restoring our republic and Constitution as "the supreme law of the land" so martial law would not last long and our constitutional foundations could be restored.)*

In the fourth and final stage of the dream, the man in black took out what looked like a new one-dollar bill, but it also looked like a cell phone. I saw George Washington's face on it, but it looked different. As I looked, someone handed me another newspaper. Its headline read, **"New Currency for a Renewed Nation."**

*(RJ: After being shown the meltdown of our economy and federal government in 1987, I studied some countries that had experienced this, like Germany in the 1930's. There are ways to restore countries, governments, and economies so they come back stronger than ever. Unfortunately, the option Germany chose "totalitarian fascism" may have quickly restored the economy but was clearly not the way to go in the long run.*

*The key for our country at that time will be our leadership. A crisis unlike any we have faced before will require a George Washington or Abraham Lincoln-like figure combined with a Moses or Apostle Paul-like figure. The Lord has promised us He will send a new generation of "founding fathers" who will fight with the same courage and resolve to restore our republic as the first ones did. Our government's restoration to its constitutional foundations is critical, which would also restore the strongest economy the world has ever known. However, for this to happen, will also require a spiritual renewal.*

*We are now entering the most troubled times in our history, yet there is also coming a restoration that will rebuild our country to its foundations of loving and honoring God and His ways. Then His favor will be restored to us. This restoration cannot happen without that. He will raise up brilliant, godly leaders for us as we had in the beginning.* "He who has begun a good work in you will complete it (see Philippians 1:6). *Never lose your hope and faith in Him.)*

The last headline handed to me read, **"Simplicity Restored as Americans Grow Their Own Food Again."**

*(RJ: We will soon see a renewed interest in the "victory gardens" of World War II when citizens of Allied nations grew so much food in their own backyards most farms were devoted to feeding the troops. This will become a matter of survival for a time, and now is the time to get started, even if on a small level. However, this also speaks of a restoration of personal resourcefulness which is crucial to our country's*

*moral, spiritual, and economic restoration. This is the only way to be the nation we are called to be and to lead the world through the coming times.)*

I believe this prophetic dream is a warning. It is one of the most vivid and intense dreams I have ever had. There are so many events in the world right now that could cause "The Perfect Storm."

I believe this dream is an unfolding of events in the near future for which we must all prepare. In fact, I believe the word "preparation" will take on a whole new meaning in the days ahead. After consulting with our leadership team, we came to some partial conclusions as to the dream's meaning. "For we know in part and we prophesy in part (I Corinthians 13:9 NKJV). No one person has the whole, but we all have a part. When we put the parts together, we will have a better perspective.

Soon you will hear more from MorningStar on how we can all prepare and equip the people of God for these coming days which seem inevitable. "Now when these things begin to happen, look up and lift up your heads, because your redemption draws near (Luke 21:28).

---

*Editors Note: While this particular dream is profound in its clarity and can easily stand alone as a springboard for prayer, it is also worth comparing with the sets of prophetic headlines independently shared by John Paul Jackson and Terry Bennett. These corollary revelations may serve as additional confirmations of some of the warnings and promises embedded in this dream.*

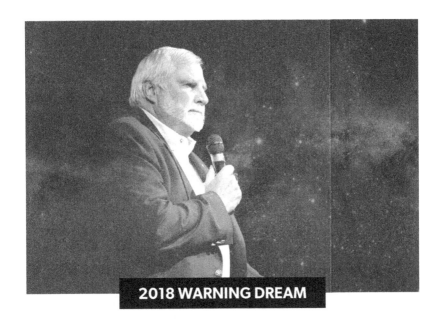

**2018 WARNING DREAM**

# "Rockets, Repentance, and Renewal"

by Rick Joyner
*Founder, MorningStar Ministries*

*This version of Rick's dream was adapted from the recounting of his 2018 dream at MorningStar University on October 10, 2023— just a few days after the Israel-Hamas war began.*

Several years ago, I had a dream that Hamas and Hezbollah started showering Israel with rockets, with the intent of overwhelming Israel's Iron Dome defense system. Their purpose for this barrage was to deplete Israel's supply of defensive rockets and so overwhelm the iron dome's capabilities that they would then be able to send in a shower of rockets that was so heavy there was no way to stop it. The barrage was really devastating to Israel.

But in the dream, I also saw in the midst of the rocket barrage, a nuclear bomb was detonated that destroyed a city in Israel.

In my dream, the city that that nuke hit was called the "wicked city." And when it hit and destroyed that city in Israel, all the rest of Israel repented and came to the Lord—all of Israel, everybody. Also, much of the world understood that this nuclear strike was evil and that it was done by terrorists, but they also knew that in a sense it could not have been allowed if God did not allow it. In the aftermath, it became widely understood that this nuclear blast was a judgment against the wicked city.

I don't know if this current war is what I saw in the dream or not. I think it could be because it looks like it's shaping up to be just what I saw in the dream. But it could also be a feint—or a test of Israel's present defenses and an attempt to deplete their defensive rockets.

I don't know if this is the beginning of the fulfillment of that dream, but if it's what I saw, I would expect in the next few days for Hezbollah to get engaged and start showering Israel with rockets from the north. Hezbollah's rockets are far more technologically advanced than what Hamas has been shooting. They can accurately target specific places in Israel. I expect them to hit Ben Gurion airport and many other very strategic places.

As I mentioned already, the city that the nuke hit was called the wicked city, and when it hit and destroyed that city in Israel, all the rest of Israel repented and came to the Lord. I have shared this dream with many people, including many people I know in Israel as well as some people in our own intelligence service. They understood right away and affirmed that this could in fact be done. Even if Iran doesn't have nukes yet, North Korea has them and could easily traffic them to Iran. As soon as I share with people that the city was called the wicked city, everyone I've spoken to immediately concludes that this city must be Tel Aviv. And it is because there's so much of what the scripture calls wickedness there. Tel Aviv is the harbors the seed of the sin and wickedness in Israel.  Some have even said that Tel Aviv at times serve as a capital for some types of wickedness for the entire world.

## A Time of Repentance and Renewal

Today, I am simply sharing the dream I was given. But if this current war is the fulfillment of that—and a city is nuked and destroyed—it's going to start the biggest harvest we have ever seen. A harvest that really is the end of this age, the reaping of more souls around the world that starts with Israel. We'll see everyone coming to the Lord and it is going to go all over the planet. Now, we've got to get engaged to do our job and to help gather in that harvest. It is a harvest that is going to be unfolding at a time of great conflict.

Ecclesiastes says, there's **"a time for war"** and **"a time for peace" (Ecclesiastes 3:8).** When it is peacetime, we need to prepare for war so we will be prepared for the time of war that is coming. War always comes. We know from the biblical prophecies about the end times: that there will be warfare until the very end of this age and only then will it be no more.  Isaiah prophesied about this:

> **"They shall beat their swords into plowshares,**
> **And their spears into pruning hooks;**
> **Nation shall not lift up sword against nation,**
> **Neither shall they learn war anymore" (Isaiah 2:4).**

At the end of this age, they'll turn their weapons into plowshares and wars will cease. But until the end of this age, there will be war and we need to be prepared for it. If it's a time for war and we're still saying, "No, it's time for peace," then we won't be ready. If you're still thinking, "It's going to be peace," you're going to be deceived and you'll be out of position.

What is being signaled right now is a time when many in the world will turn against the terrorists—against radical Islam. This kind of thing cannot be acceptable. It cannot be tolerated in our land. Now I say there are extremes on everything. There are many faces to Islam and many in Islam hate what went on with what Hamas is doing as much as everybody else. Some of the Muslims who don't support this are going to pay a terrible price for it. In many ways, they already are paying a terrible price. While we cannot judge everybody by the externals, it also is not possible to defeat an enemy that we cannot recognize. In order to win this battle at home and abroad, we have to recognize the enemy of radical Jihadist Islam and defeat it.

Now, if great revival and harvest breaks out, you are going to immediately find yourselves in full-time ministry. Do you understand that? We all are: It's "all hands on deck." It's about getting engaged. There is nothing more important in world history than what we've been called to be a part of. We want to be ready for it and until that day happens we will do all we can to prepare you to overcome in the midst of what is unfolding.

***

### *Editorial Note from Michael Fickess*

*I have personally heard Rick share this dream in private many times over the last few years, including at our MSU Masters in Leadership program. So when I heard him share this dream with our students only days after the war, I knew it was important to share it more widely. This recap of his 2018 dream was shared only days after the Israel-Hamas war began after Hamas launched a major terror attack against Israel, but before any of the other events in the dream were fulfilled (Israel's conflict with Hezbollah began to accelerate just days after Rick shared his dream again with us on October 10, 2023)*

**PROPHETIC MESSAGE**

# The Spiritual Resurgence of the Prince of Persia

## (with Additional Prophecies for Nations)

by Chris Reed,
*President of MorningStar*

*Chris shared the following prophetic message on October 21, 2023, at MorningStar Ministries' Advanced Prophetic Conference.*

In Daniel chapter 10, we see that Daniel had been fasting and praying for 21 days when an angel showed up to explain what was happening in the second heaven, where the archangel Michael was wrestling with a demonic principality called, the "Prince of Persia."

**12 Then he said to me, "Do not fear, Daniel, for from the first day that you set your heart to understand and to humble**

yourself before your God, your words were heard, and I have come because of your words.

13 But the prince of the kingdom of Persia withstood me twenty-one days; and behold, Michael, one of the chief princes, came to help me, for I had been left alone there with the kings of Persia.

14 Now I have come to make you understand what will happen to your people in the latter days, for the vision *refers* to *many* days yet *to come.*"—Daniel 10:12-14

This passage describes a demonic principality that was called the "Prince of Persia." This is the spirit that was driving the Medes and the Persians to destroy Babylon in ancient times. It was the principality that Daniel warred against through prayer and fasting for 21 days. And from day one, he prayed and the angel was sent from the third heaven and wrestled with that principality over Persia in the second heaven for as long as Daniel was praying.

The demonic principality of the Prince of Persia is resurfacing today. It is the same spirit that's influencing Iran right now, as it funds Hamas and Hezbollah in acts of terror against Israel. It's the same spirit at work—just a different millennium.

Let's look at some other passages to see what this principality that drove the Medes and Persians is capable of releasing. Isaiah 13 tells us:

15 Everyone who is found will be thrust through, and everyone who is captured will fall by the sword.

16 Their children also will be dashed to pieces before their eyes; their houses will be plundered and their wives ravished.

162

**¹⁷ "Behold, I will stir up the Medes against them, who will not regard silver; and *as for* gold, they will not delight in it.**

**¹⁸ Also *their* bows will dash the young men to pieces, and they will have no pity on the fruit of the womb; their eye will not spare children.**

The details in this passage are terrifying, and yet we saw this very thing unfold in Israel when Hamas terrorists attacked. Verse 15 warns, "everyone who is found will be thrust through": when Hamas attacked, they killed anyone they could find—little kids, the elderly, and young families. There was a demonic rage to what happened. The next verse warns, "their children will be dashed to pieces" and we saw the horrific evidence of infants and toddlers beheaded by Hamas right in front of their parents in many cases. The same verse warns about "their wives [being] ravished" and we also saw Hamas raping women—both at the time they attacked small Israeli border villages as well as the women they kidnapped as hostages and brought back into Gaza.

This isn't normal human behavior, not even for soldiers in a time of war—it's evil and demonic behavior. The spirit that is manifesting through Hamas and through radical Islam right now is the same spirit that drove Israel's enemies to madness thousands of years ago. What we're seeing today is the spiritual resurgence of the Prince of Persia.

I don't hate the Iranian people: we love the Iranian people and we love the Palestinian people. But we are going to have to wrestle with radical Islam and that includes wrestling with their principality of Persia that is rising up again in the Middle East and even trying to influence other places in the world.

# Additional Prophetic Words for Nations

We need to be able to interpret revelation in times of crisis just as Daniel did. God is raising up a company of people who can receive revelation, interpret it, apply it, know who to share it with, know if they're supposed to share it and know the timing of when they're supposed to share it. Now, I'm going to share some more things I was shown. These are prophecies that you will see come to pass and you will see these events covered by the news.

## a. Arms Sales Involving Russia, Iran, and Ukraine

There will be a swap of arms to Iran from Russia in exchange for neighborhood warfare drones. And that's what's going to happen in Ukraine. The Russians are going to use drone warfare in exchange for giving Iran weapons of war—and we've seen those weapons.

Russia's support of Iran will be exposed, including giving them arms. Iran will also be exposed for supporting Hamas and Hezbollah. Somehow, Iran has found a way to use the money — or the reimbursement—that came from U.S. government funding. Biden will not condemn Iran because he knows he is vulnerable.

## b. Middle East War Escalation

The Israel-Hamas war will extend into Lebanon. They will plunder the Gaza strip, but there will also be attacks on the West Bank and the Golan Heights in northern Israel. We'll also see attacks from the north, the east, and the south.

We'll see it come from Lebanon, Syria, and Hamas, but you're also going to see Iran get hit big. I've prophesied about Israel

164

suddenly striking Iran (see prophecy #28 in this book). I see it happening in the mountains of Iran. I saw a nuclear development plant. Iran is going to get hit big because Israel knows who is funding and supporting Hamas.

### c. Islamic Terrorism Spreading

You're going to see a resurgence of Islamic terrorism this year and even more into next year. Just as I prophesied last year that it would happen in Germany and Sweden and it's happened in the last month, now you're going to see it in the U.K., Germany, France, and Sweden.

Islamic terrorism is going to spread and a lot of it will be because of mass illegal immigration coming up from the southern hemisphere to the northern hemisphere. This is not just happening in America. Mass illegal immigration is flowing from Africa and the Middle East into Europe, just as mass illegal immigration is flowing from South and Central America up into North America.

And Poland will be in the news again, as I prophesied two years ago about a political swing from left to right. And you'll also see another downed aircraft from Poland. These are the things I have been shown.

### d. A Four-Fold Cord with China, North Korea, Iran, and Russia

China will make advances toward Taiwan. You're going to read and hear about some sort of downed war vessel in the sea. You're going to see China, North Korea, Iran, and Russia form a four-fold cord. This will be out of desperation. With what's going on in the Russia-Ukraine war, they're hoping that the world will only see what's happening in the Middle East now.

165

We care about what is happening in the Middle East because we love Israel, but let me tell you something: we cannot let the enemy get us focused exclusively on the Middle East because there are also atrocities that have been taking place in Eastern Europe for nearly two years now.

## e. 2024 is a Critical Year for America

Hear me now—even if you haven't heard anything else I've said tonight: The 2024 election will decide what kind of nation we will be for the rest of our existence. If it goes wrong, we will never recover. I know that warning comes from the Lord and it is serious. If the election goes wrong, we will never be the traditional America we once were—the "city on a hill" that President Reagan said we were.

I'm sorry if you don't like Trump, but imagine another year or more of this. God is not done with Donald Trump. Don't throw in the towel on him. Don't walk away from people who fought for Israel and fought for America and established the embassy in Jerusalem. I'm not saying what I'm saying because it makes me popular. I'm not saying it because somebody's trying to tell me to say it. I'm saying this because America is the greatest nation and it deserves to be fought for. We need preachers to preach in the pulpit and tell their congregations to get out and vote and make a difference.

## f. Jimmy Carter's Death Will Be a Sign

*As recorded on the Lance Wallnau Show (January 21, 2023)*

I have shared this with my team privately, but this is the first time I've shared this publicly. So this is a new prophecy that I have already shared with Rick and with some others that I trust.

This is the latest encounter that I had with the lord in the second week of January this year and it came in a trance or a vision. During the encounter, I was taken into the Capital Rotunda in Washington, D.C. This is the place where many times national figures lie "in state" to be honored after they have passed away. Presidents and other high-profile national leaders often lie in state there when they die. In this encounter, it was a funeral and I walked up, and I saw the casket of someone in the capital rotunda: it was former President Jimmy Carter lying in state.

And you know, it was because of natural causes because he is already advanced in years. Since he's in his 90s now, that's not a great surprise. But there was a note that was on the casket at the end of the casket and it said that the death of Jimmy Carter would be a marker in time. When I saw this, I saw that the natural death of Jimmy Carter would be a signpost that pointed to the "death" of the Biden Administration.

# APPENDIX 3:

# Documenting the 40 Prophecies

The following pages offer samples of some of the screenshots from Chris Reed's notes on his mobile phone. This documentation is important because it demonstrates that in many cases, Chris received these words prophetically long before leading indicators would be visible. In addition to being referenced in this book, Chris has described this documentation in great detail on MorningStarTV.

MORNINGSTAR**TV**⟩

**Scan the QR code to watch Chris explain the documentation for the 40 prophecies in detail on MorningStarTV.**

**Above:** Chris' prophecies are logged and time-stamped on the Notes app of his phone. This documents the time frame for when the Lord gave each word, which in many cases happened years in advance. The date and time of each note are preserved unless changes are made to the note.

**Right:** The date and time is visible on this note because it has not been "scrolled down". Some of screenshots on the following pages may not include the date and time stamp because they were taken after scrolling down to read them. However, you can view the time stamps on the MSTV video when Chris explains them.

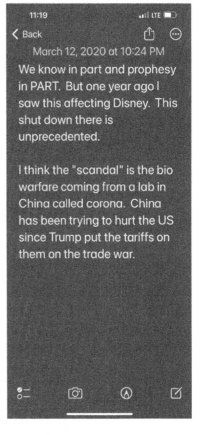

11:19       ..ll LTE ⬛

< Back       ⬆ ⋯

March 12, 2020 at 10:24 PM

We know in part and prophesy in PART. But one year ago I saw this affecting Disney. This shut down there is unprecedented.

I think the "scandal" is the bio warfare coming from a lab in China called corona. China has been trying to hurt the US since Trump put the tariffs on them on the trade war.

**Below:** Category 1—Some of Chris' notes simply document the prophecies that have already been shared throughout this book.

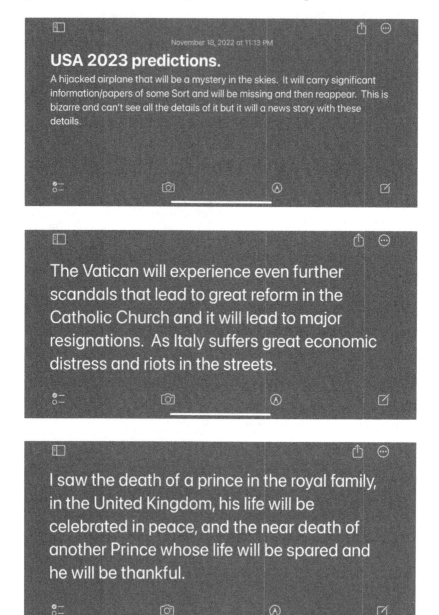

November 18, 2022 at 11:13 PM

**USA 2023 predictions.**

A hijacked airplane that will be a mystery in the skies. It will carry significant information/papers of some Sort and will be missing and then reappear. This is bizarre and can't see all the details of it but it will a news story with these details.

The Vatican will experience even further scandals that lead to great reform in the Catholic Church and it will lead to major resignations. As Italy suffers great economic distress and riots in the streets.

I saw the death of a prince in the royal family, in the United Kingdom, his life will be celebrated in peace, and the near death of another Prince whose life will be spared and he will be thankful.

Some of Chris' notes include revelations that have not been shared as widely as the 40 prophecies, but have come to pass nonetheless.

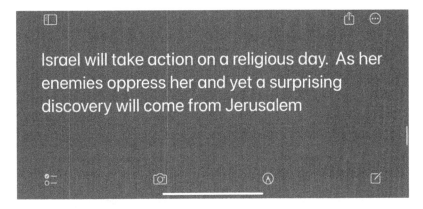

**Above:** This important sign prophecy came to pass when Hamas attacked Israel on the "last and greatest day" of the Feast of Tabernacles.

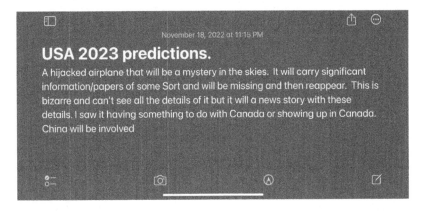

**Above:** Although this word was not widely publicized, it came to pass with precision when a Chinese spy balloon came into American air space through Canada and crossed the entire continental United States before being shot down over the Atlantic Ocean. It made national headlines at the time.

**Below:** Some of Chris' notes include revelations that have not been shared widely and also have yet to be fulfilled.

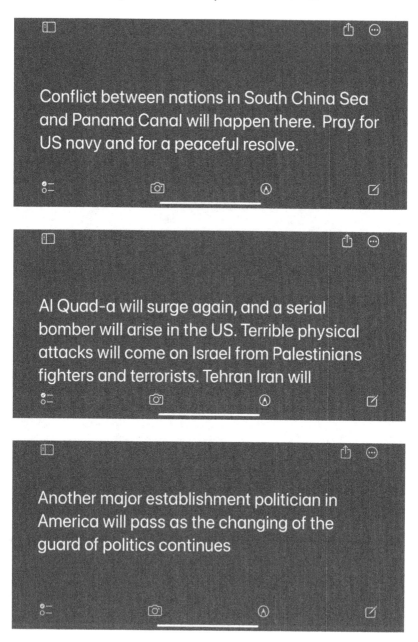

Conflict between nations in South China Sea and Panama Canal will happen there. Pray for US navy and for a peaceful resolve.

Al Quad-a will surge again, and a serial bomber will arise in the US. Terrible physical attacks will come on Israel from Palestinians fighters and terrorists. Tehran Iran will

Another major establishment politician in America will pass as the changing of the guard of politics continues

# BIBLIOGRAPHY

Adler, Katya. "Far-Right Parties on the Rise across Europe." *BBC News*, 30 June 2023, www.bbc.com/news/world-europe-66056375. Accessed 13 Oct. 2023.

Altus, K. (2023, July 28). GOP Rep. Nancy Mace claims Biden family received over $50M from influence peddling scheme. Fox Business. https://www.foxbusiness.com/politics/gop-rep-nancy-mace-claims-biden-family-recieved-influence-peddling-scheme. Accessed 10 Oct. 2023.

Ainsley, Julia. "Number of People on Terror Watchlist Stopped at U.S. Border Has Risen." *NBC News*, 14 Sept. 2023, www.nbcnews.com/politics/national-security/number-people-terror-watchlist-stopped-mexico-us-border-risen-rcna105095. Accessed 11 Oct. 2023.

Aitken, Peter, and Fox News. "Netanyahu Readies Strike on Iran Nuclear Facilities: Report." *New York Post*, 23 Feb. 2023, nypost.com/2023/02/23/netanyahu-readies-strike-on-iran-nuclear-facilities-report/. Accessed 16 Oct. 2023.

Altuntaş, Atila. "Sweden Grapples with Surge in Gang-Related Violence." Www.aa.com.tr, 30 Sept. 2023, www.aa.com.tr/en/europe/sweden-grapples-with-surge-in-gang-related-violence/3004365. Accessed 13 Oct. 2023.

Amnesty International. "The Hidden History of China's Protest Movement." *Amnesty International*, 1 June 2023, www.amnesty.org/en/latest/news/2023/06/right-to-peaceful-protest-in-china-on-tiananmen-anniversary/. Accessed 17 Oct. 2023.

Archive, View Author, and Get author RSS feed. "Just 3% of San Francisco Restaurants Have Not Been Vandalized: Survey." *News York Post*, 28 Sept. 2023, nypost.com/2023/09/28/just-3-of-san-francisco-restaurants-have-not-been-vandalized-survey/. Accessed 10 Oct. 2023.

Asadu, Chinedu. "UN: Millions Left with No Aid as West Africa Suffers Worst Hunger Crisis in 10 Years." *AP News*, 5 July 2023, apnews.com/article/un-food-west-africa-hunger-aid-conflict-3bac5025cc26ed59318bbf63c2e02626. Accessed 12 Oct. 2023.

Askew, Joshua. "'Keep Ireland Irish': Say Hello to Ireland's Growing Far Right." *Euronews*, 13 Mar. 2023, www.euronews.com/2023/03/13/keep-ireland-irish-say-hello-to-irelands-growing-far-right. Accessed 13 Oct. 2023.

Associated Press. "France Riots Enter Fifth Night, over 700 Arrested on Day of Teenager's Funeral." *New York Post*, 2 July 2023, nypost.com/2023/07/02/france-riots-enter-fifth-night-over-700-arrested-on-day-of-teenagers-funeral/. Accessed 15 Oct. 2023.

—. "Mobs of Masked Teens Ransacked Philadelphia Stores. Police Have Made over a Dozen Arrests." *AP News*, 27 Sept. 2023, apnews.com/article/philadelphia-store-mob-thefts-teenagers-f2351d631f691aa081233b1df1bee54d.

Ballesteros, Aldrin. "Fentanyl Seizures at the Southwest Border: A Breakdown by CBP Areas of Responsibility | Wilson Center." www.wilsoncenter.org, 29 Aug. 2023, www.wilsoncenter.org/article/fentanyl-seizures-southwest-border-breakdown-cbp-areas-responsibility#:~:text=Fentanyl%20seizures%20at%20the%20Mexico. Accessed 11 Oct. 2023.

BBC. "Ukraine War: Putin Confirms First Nuclear Weapons Moved to Belarus." *BBC News*, 16 June 2023, www.bbc.com/news/world-europe-65932700. Accessed 16 Oct. 2023.

BBC News . "Bank of China Fraud: Italy Seeks Trial for 300 People." *BBC News*, 21 June 2015, www.bbc.com/news/world-europe-33214450. Accessed 17 Oct. 2023.

Boak, Josh, and Hannah Fingerhut. "Biden 2024? Most Democrats Say No Thank You: AP-NORC Poll." *AP NEWS*, 6 Feb. 2023, apnews.com/article/ap-norc-poll-biden-2024-presidential-prospects-c843c5af6775b4c8a0cff8e2b1db03f6. Accessed 12 Oct. 2023.

Boffey, Daniel, and Daniel Boffey Chief reporter. "Solar-Powered Off-Road Car Finishes 620-Mile Test Drive across North Africa." *The Guardian*, 16 Oct. 2023, www.theguardian.com/environment/2023/oct/16/solar-powered-off-road-car-stella-terra-finishes-620-mile-test-drive-across-north-africa. Accessed 17 Oct. 2023.

Borelli, Joe. "Democrats Seeing Sense on the Border Crisis, Welcome to the (Grand Old) Party!" *New York Post*, 5 Oct. 2023, nypost.com/2023/10/05/democrats-seeing-sense-on-the-border-crisis-welcome-to-the-grand-old-party/. Accessed 11 Oct. 2023.

Borland, Ben. "Is the Real Stone of Destiny Going to Be Used for King Charles's Coronation." *Scottish Daily Express*, 12 Oct. 2022, www.scottishdailyexpress.co.uk/news/uk-news/real-stone-destiny-going-used-28220208. Accessed 17 Oct. 2023.

Camarota, Steven. "What the Media Tell You about Illegal-Immigrant Crime Is Plain Wrong." *New York Post*, 20 Oct. 2022, nypost.com/2022/10/19/what-the-media-tell-you-about-illegal-immigrant-crime-is-plain-wrong/. Accessed 20 Oct. 2023.

Castor, Rebekah. "Mexican Cartels' Drug Dealings 'Top Priority' as Fentanyl Pours across Southern Border, DEA Says." *Fox News*, 29 June 2023, www.foxnews.com/us/mexican-cartels-drug-dealings-top-priority-fentanyl-pours-across-southern-border-dea. Accessed 20 Oct. 2023.

Charlton, Angela, and Jeffrey Schaeffer. "France Has Banned Pro-Palestinian Protests and Vowed to Protect Jews from Resurgent Antisemitism." *AP News*, 12 Oct. 2023, apnews.com/article/france-israel-palestinians-war-protests-banned-5626bafec480b32226dcb97d0c92a553. Accessed 14 Oct. 2023.

CHOI, JOSEPH. "A Third of Adults Believe COVID-19 Vaccines Caused Thousands of Sudden Deaths: Poll." *The Hill*, 22 Aug. 2023, thehill.com/policy/healthcare/4162874-a-third-of-adults-believe-covid-19-vaccines-caused-thousands-of-sudden-deaths-poll/. Accessed 21 Sept. 2023.

COOK, LORNE. "Angered over EU Migrant Rules, Poland and Hungary Veto a Summit Statement in a Gesture of Protest." *AP News*, 29 June 2023, apnews.com/article/eu-poland-hungary-migration-refugees-relocation-cf75417b7a9490c3a41216478200c9e0. Accessed 14 Oct. 2023.

COPP, TARA. "What We Know about the Marine Corps F-35 Crash, Backyard Ejection and What Went Wrong." *AP News*, 19 Sept. 2023, apnews.com/article/f35-crash-military-marines-plane-0a99d551aeff9eeab1a105215d7f203d. Accessed 10 Oct. 2023.

Dailymail. "Thousands of 'Special Interest Aliens' Tried to Enter US." *Mail Online*, 11 Oct. 2023, www.dailymail.co.uk/news/article-12618757/border-special-aliens-iran-afghanistan.html. Accessed 19 Oct. 2023.

Devine, Miranda. "Allegations against Biden and His Family Are Too Credible to Wipe Away with 'Father's Love' Sob Story." *New York Post*, 29 June 2023, nypost.com/2023/06/28/allegations-against-biden-and-his-family-are-too-credible-to-wipe-away-with-fathers-love-sob-story/. Accessed 11 Oct. 2023.

Dickie, Gloria. "Hurricane Idalia: How Climate Change Is Fueling Hurricanes." *Reuters*, 30 Aug. 2023, www.reuters.com/world/us/how-climate-change-is-fueling-hurricanes-2023-08-30/.

Dixon-Hamilton, Jordan. "'Failed Progressive Utopia': Oakland Residents Demand City Act on Crime." *Breitbart*, 1 June 2023, www.breitbart.com/politics/2023/05/31/failed-progressive-utopia-oakland-residents-demand-city-act-rising-crime/. Accessed 10 Oct. 2023.

Doherty, Erin. "What We Know about the Biden Classified Documents Investigation." *Axios*, 1 Feb. 2023, www.axios.com/2023/01/12/biden-classified-documents-timeline. Accessed 12 Oct. 2023.

Donlevy, Katherine. "Murders Jumped 10% since 2021 in Mostly Blue States: Study." *New York Post*, 27 Apr. 2023, nypost.com/2023/04/26/murders-jumped-10-since-2021-in-mostly-blue-states-study/. Accessed 20 Oct. 2023.

Doornbos, Caitlin. "Suella Braverman Warns of 'Unsustainable' Crisis as Illegal Migration Booms." *New York Post*, 26 Sept. 2023, nypost.com/2023/09/25/suella-braverman-warns-of-unsustainable-crisis-as-illegal-migration-booms/. Accessed 13 Oct. 2023.

Eldridge, Stacey. "'Completely Lost and Very Depressed': Prince Andrew in 'Bad Shape.'" *Skynews*, 8 Nov. 2022, www.skynews.com.au/world-news/united-kingdom/completely-lost-and-depressed-prince-andrew-in-bad-shape-after-king-charles-told-him-hed-never-resume-his-royal-duties/news-story/99c0c31acdbe7dfde4d95f1bfa1767ea#. Accessed 16 Oct. 2023.

Fleck, Anna. "Infographic: Sweden's Deadly Gun Violence." *Statista Daily Data*, 2 Oct. 2023, www.statista.com/chart/30946/annual-number-of-fatal-shootings-in-sweden/. Accessed 13 Oct. 2023.

Frazin, Rachel. "What Does the Israel-Hamas Conflict Mean for Oil Prices?" *The Hill*, 9 Oct. 2023, thehill.com/policy/energy-environment/4246506-what-does-the-israel-hamas-conflict-mean-for-oil-prices/. Accessed 10 Oct. 2023.

GANLEY, ELAINE. "France's Anti-Immigration Far Right Gets Boost from Riots over Police Killing of Teen." *AP News*, 12 July 2023, apnews.com/article/france-police-shooting-far-right-85adc47ce3e6982879b391fcd84758e9. Accessed 14 Oct. 2023.

Giuffrida, Angela. "'She Plays the Moderate but Winks at Those Who Are Not': The Many Faces of Giorgia Meloni." *The Guardian*, 21 Sept. 2023, www.theguardian.com/world/2023/sep/21/many-faces-of-giorgia-meloni-year-in-power-italy-prime-minister. Accessed 17 Oct. 2023.

Goodyear, Sheena. "Scottish Stone Shouldn't Be in Coronation, Says Son of Man Who Stole It Back from England." *CBC*, 8 May 2023, www.cbc.ca/radio/asithappens/stone-of-destiny-1950-heist-1.6833819. Accessed 17 Oct. 2023.

Gosling, Tim. "Nationalist, Populist, Far-Right Parties Eye Rising Support across Europe." Www.aljazeera.com, 20 Sept. 2023, www.aljazeera.com/features/2023/9/20/nationalist-populist-far-right-parties-eye-rising-support-across-europe. Accessed 13 Oct. 2023.

Hagstrom, Anders. "China Deploys over 40 Planes to Taiwan Strait, Is Massing Forces at Coastal Military Bases, Taiwan Warns." *Fox News*, 12 Sept. 2023, www.foxnews.com/world/china-deploys-40-planes-taiwan-strait-massing-forces-coastal-military-bases-taiwan-warns.

Harper, Casey. "Sanctuary Cities Have Regrets as Flood of Illegal Migrants Continues." *The Center Square*, 23 July 2023, www.thecentersquare.com/national/article_d8377298-27f0-11ee-8f11-e76c5492baff.html. Accessed 20 Oct. 2023.

Hauf, Patrick. "1.5 Million 'Gotaways' at the Border under the Biden Administration: Report." *Fox News*, 16 May 2023, www.foxnews.com/politics/million-gotaways-border-biden-administration-report. Accessed 20 Oct. 2023.

He, Laura. "China's Economy Will Be Hobbled for Years by the Real Estate Crisis | CNN Business." *CNN*, 6 Oct. 2023, www.cnn.com/2023/10/06/economy/china-economy-real-estate-crisis-intl-hnk/index.html. Accessed 17 Oct. 2023.

Hill, Thomas. "Food Prices in Spain Expected to Rise due to Crop Failure." *Euronews*, 19 Apr. 2023, www.euronews.com/2023/04/19/drought-threatens-grain-harvests-in-spain. Accessed 16 Oct. 2023.

IBRAHIM, SAMANTHA. "Epstein Victim: My Friend Was Forced to Have Sex with Prince Andrew." *New York Post* , 21 Aug. 2023, nypost.com/2023/08/21/epstein-victim-my-friend-was-forced-to-have-sex-with-prince-andrew/. Accessed 16 Oct. 2023.

India Today. "Iran Trying to Deploy Weapons in Syria to Open New War Front: Israeli Official." *India Today*, 15 Oct. 2023, www.indiatoday.in/world/story/israel-joshua-zarka-head-of-strategic-affairs-foreign-ministry-iran-arms-to-syria-hezbollah-aleppo-airport-2449245-2023-10-15. Accessed 16 Oct. 2023.

Interrante, Abbey. "February 2023 – Solar Cycle 25." Blogs.nasa.gov, 17 Feb. 2023, blogs.nasa.gov/solarcycle25/2023/02/#:~:text=The%20Sun%20emitted%20a%20strong%20solar%20flare%2C%20peaking%20at%2010. Accessed 16 Oct. 2023.

JERUSALEM POST STAFF. "Iran 'Gave Green Light,' Helped Plan Hamas Massacre - WSJ." *The Jerusalem Post* | JPost.com, 9 Oct. 2023, www.jpost.com/breaking-news/article-765286. Accessed 16 Oct. 2023.

Jha, Somesh. "Is a Global Food Crisis the New Normal?" Www.aljazeera.com, 29 Aug. 2023, www.aljazeera.com/features/2023/8/29/is-a-global-food-crisis-the-new-normal. Accessed 12 Oct. 2023.

Jones, Allie. "Harry and Meghan Are Not Getting Divorced and They Want You to Know All about It." *The Cut*, 8 Aug. 2023, www.thecut.com/2023/08/prince-harry-meghan-divorce-rumors.html. Accessed 17 Oct. 2023.

KARNOWSKI, STEVE. "Deadly Bird Flu Reappears in US Commercial Poultry Flocks in Utah and South Dakota." *AP News*, 10 Oct. 2023, apnews.com/article/bird-flu-avian-influenza-outbreak-virus-7b83ed4d76607bf874685e84b969ceae. Accessed 16 Oct. 2023.

Kent, Simon. "Blinken Meets Xi as China Warns U.S. Must Choose between 'Cooperation or Conflict.'" *Breitbart*, 19 June 2023, www.breitbart.com/asia/2023/06/19/blinken-to-meet-xi-as-china-warns-u-s-must-choose-between-cooperation-or-conflict-with-beijing/. Accessed 10 Oct. 2023.

Klee, Miles. "Claims of Covid Vaccine Injuries and Deaths Revive Protest Movement." *Rolling Stone*, 24 Jan. 2023, www.rollingstone.com/culture/culture-features/anti-vax-movement-new-misinformation-injuries-deaths-1234666611/. Accessed 17 Oct. 2023.

Koenig, Melissa. "Illegal Crossings of Migrant Families at US-Mexico Border Hits All-Time High." *New York Post*, 1 Sept. 2023, nypost.com/2023/09/01/illegal-crossings-of-migrant-families-at-us-mexico-border-hits-all-time-high/. Accessed 12 Oct. 2023.

Kozul-Wright , Alex. "Year of War in Ukraine Left Developing Nations Picking up Pieces." Www.aljazeera.com, 19 Feb. 2023, www.aljazeera.com/economy/2023/2/19/a-year-of-war-in-ukraine-has-left-developing-countries-picking-up-pieces. Accessed 11 Oct. 2023.

Kurilla, Michelle. "The President's Inbox Recap: The Israel-Hamas War." *Council on Foreign Relations*, 13 Oct. 2023, www.cfr.org/blog/presidents-inbox-recap-israel-hamas-war. Accessed 16 Oct. 2023.

Langmaid, Virginia. "Multiple Structural Problems Caused Davenport, Iowa, Apartment Building Collapse That Killed 3 Residents, Investigation Finds." *CNN*, 8 Sept. 2023, www.cnn.com/2023/09/07/us/davenport-iowa-building-collapse-investigation/index.html#:~:text=Search%20and%20rescue%20efforts%20continued. Accessed 10 Oct. 2023.

Lee, Medora. "Higher Food Bills? Your Veggies, Nuts and Berries May Cost More Thanks to Extreme Weather." *USA TODAY*, 5 May 2023, www.usatoday.com/story/money/economy/2023/05/05/extreme-2023-weather-food-prices-selection/70172578007/. Accessed 16 Oct. 2023.

LIGHTMAN, DAVID. "Gavin Newsom Denies White House Bid, but He Is Following the Contender's Playbook." *The Sacramento Bee*, 7 Aug. 2023, www.sacbee.com/news/politics-government/election/presidential-election/article277938603.html. Accessed 12 Oct. 2023.

Liu, Xiaoke (Ken). "Young Athletes and Heart Health." *Mayo Clinic Health System*, 25 Jan. 2023, www.mayoclinichealthsystem.org/hometown-health/speaking-of-health/young-athletes-and-heart-health#:~:text=Sudden%20cardiac%20arrest%20is%20the. Accessed 17 Oct. 2023.

MAADDI, ROB. "Damar Hamlin Put Prayer in Football Back in the Spotlight." *AP NEWS*, 9 Feb. 2023, apnews.com/article/damar-hamlin-prayer-football-super-bowl-76d687691c649b702a584a5957d1f4f3. Accessed 17 Oct. 2023.

Maaddi, Rob. "EXPLAINER: What Happened to Damar Hamlin?" *AP NEWS*, 3 Jan. 2023, apnews.com/article/Bills-damar-hamlin-collapse-what-happened-d73a76f2f7f736b652e95896dfaa0900. Accessed 17 Oct. 2023.

Malik, Tariq. "The Sun Just Erupted with a Major X-Class Solar Flare. Here's What It Looked like on Video." Space.com, 12 Feb. 2023, www.space.com/sun-erupts-huge-x-class-solar-flare-february-2023. Accessed 16 Oct. 2023.

MARCA. "Meghan and Harry's Strategy for Handling Separation Rumors Revealed." *MARCA*, 20 July 2023, www.marca.com/en/lifestyle/celebrities/2023/07/20/64b924ceca474154248b459b.html. Accessed 17 Oct. 2023.

Martinez, MaryAnn. "Texas Gov Claims He's Stopped Enough Fentanyl to Kill Entire US in Latest Battle with Biden." *New York Post*, 24 July 2023, nypost.com/2023/07/24/texas-gov-claims-hes-stopped-enough-fentanyl-to-kill-entire-us-in-latest-battle-with-biden/. Accessed 19 Oct. 2023.

Matthews, Merrill. "Suspected Terrorists Are Streaming across Biden's Broken Border." *The Hill*, 26 Sept. 2023, thehill.com/opinion/immigration/4223357-suspected-terrorists-are-streaming-across-bidens-broken-border/. Accessed 19 Oct. 2023.

Maynes, Charles. "Putin Accuses Wagner Group of a Treasonous 'Military Uprising' in Russia." *NPR*, 24 June 2023, www.npr.org/2023/06/24/1184147525/putin-wagner-treason-rebellion. Accessed 17 Oct. 2023.

Melugin, Bill, and Adam Shaw. "Thousands of 'Special Interest Aliens' from Middle East Countries Stopped at Southern Border since 2021: Data." *Fox News*, 10 Oct. 2023, www.foxnews.com/politics/thousands-special-interest-aliens-middle-east-countries-stopped-southern-border-2021-data. Accessed 19 Oct. 2023.

Miller, Andrew. "Hamas Attacks Reminder That Sleeper Cells Are Crossing Southern Border, Expert Warns: 'They're Already Here.'" *Fox News*, 10 Oct. 2023, www.foxnews.com/politics/hamas-attack-reminder-sleeper-cells-crossing-southern-border-expert-warns-theyre-already-here. Accessed 20 Oct. 2023.

MUNSTER, BEN. "The Mysterious Swindling of the EU and the Bank of Italy." *POLITICO*, 16 June 2023, www.politico.eu/article/bank-of-italy-eesc-banker-fraud-case/. Accessed 17 Oct. 2023.

Myers, Megan. "Border under Control of Cartels, Not the US, Yuma Residents Say as Gangs Rake in Billions off Human Smuggling." *Fox News*, 16 Jan. 2023, www.foxnews.com/us/border-control-cartels-us-yuma-residents-say-gangs-rake-billions-human-smuggling. Accessed 19 Oct. 2023.

Nava, Victor. "James Comer Demands Penn Biden Center Visitor Logs, China Donor Info." *New York Post*, 19 Jan. 2023, nypost.com/2023/01/18/james-comer-demands-penn-biden-center-visitor-logs-china-donor-info/. Accessed 12 Oct. 2023.

NBC News. "Climate Change and NYC: Historic Rains Buckle City's Infrastructure, Again." *NBC News*, 29 Sept. 2023, www.nbcnews.com/science/environment/nyc-flooding-climate-change-infrastructure-limitations-rcna118170. Accessed 21 Oct., 2023.

Nehamas, Nicholas. "DeSantis Amps up Attacks on Trump, as G.O.P. Primary Enters a New Phase." *The New York Times*, 10 Oct. 2023, www.nytimes.com/2023/10/10/us/politics/desantis-trump-2024.html. Accessed 11 Oct. 2023.

Nelson, Steven. "WH Admits More Classified Docs Found in Biden's Delaware Garage." *News York Post*, 12 Jan. 2023, nypost.com/2023/01/12/wh-admits-more-classified-docs-found-in-bidens-delaware-garage/. Accessed 12 Oct. 2023.

Nolte, John. "Nolte: Democrat-Run Chicago Year-To-Date Crime Rate up 97% Compared to 2021." *Breitbart*, 26 Jan. 2023, www.breitbart.com/politics/2023/01/26/nolte-democrat-run-chicago-year-to-date-crime-rate-up-97-compared-to-2021/. Accessed 10 Oct. 2023.

Norman, Greg. "Hezbollah Takes Responsibility for Attacks on Israeli Military Posts along Lebanon Border." *Fox News*, 13 Oct. 2023, www.foxnews.com/world/hezbollah-takes-responsibility-attacks-israeli-military-posts-along-lebanon-border. Accessed 16 Oct. 2023.

O'Neill, Jesse. "Iran Can Make Enough Fissile for One Nuke in 12 Days: US." *New York Post*, 1 Mar. 2023, nypost.com/2023/03/01/iran-can-make-enough-fissile-for-one-nuclear-bomb-in-just-12-days-official-says/. Accessed 16 Oct. 2023.

Olorunnipa, Toluse, et al. "Anxiety Ripples through the Democratic Party over Biden." *Washington Post*, 19 Sept. 2023, www.washingtonpost.com/nation/2023/09/18/biden-democrats-anxiety-age/#:~:text=. Accessed 9 Oct. 2023.

Paddison, Nadeen Ebrahim,Laura. "Aging Dams and Missed Warnings: A Lethal Mix of Factors Caused Africa's Deadliest Flood Disaster." *CNN*, 14 Sept. 2023, www.cnn.com/2023/09/14/middleeast/lethal-factors-leading-to-libya-floods-intl/index.html. Accessed 10 Oct. 2023.

Pennington, Josh, et al. "Medvedev Says Russia Could Use Nuclear Weapon If Ukraine's Fightback Succeeds in Latest Threat." *CNN*, 31 July 2023, www.cnn.com/2023/07/31/europe/medvedev-russia-nuclear-weapons-intl-hnk/index.html. Accessed 16 Oct. 2023.

Radowitz , Bernd. "Chinese Green Power Executive Arrested in Germany ahead of World's Biggest Solar Event." *Recharge | Latest Renewable Energy News*, 13 June 2023, www.rechargenews.com/energy-transition/chinese-green-power-executive-arrested-in-germany-ahead-of-worlds-biggest-solar-event/2-1-1466740. Accessed 14 Oct. 2023.

Rahman, Khaleda. "New York City Will Be Destroyed by Migrant Influx—Eric Adams." *Newsweek*, 7 Sept. 2023, www.newsweek.com/eric-adams-migrant-influx-destroy-new-york-city-1825250. Accessed 20 Oct. 2023.

Real Clear Politics. "RealClearPolitics - Election Other - President Biden Job Approval." Www.realclearpolitics.com, 12 Oct. 2023, www.realclearpolitics.com/epolls/other/president-biden-job-approval-7320.html. Accessed 12 Oct. 2023.

Reed, Betsy. "Sweden Hit by 'Unprecedented' Levels of Gang Violence." *The Guardian*, 13 Sept. 2023, www.theguardian.com/world/2023/sep/13/sweden-gang-violence-shootings-explosions. Accessed 13 Oct. 2023.

Reid, Tim, and Nathan Layne. "Insight: Trump Is Attacking DeSantis Hard on Policy, amid the Flurry of Insults." *Reuters*, 17 May 2023, www.reuters.com/world/us/trump-is-attacking-desantis-hard-policy-amid-flurry-insults-2023-05-17/. Accessed 11 Oct. 2023.

Reuters. "Biden Says Climate Crisis Is Undeniable after Hurricane Idalia Damage." *Reuters*, 30 Aug. 2023, www.reuters.com/world/us/biden-says-climate-crisis-is-undeniable-after-hurricane-idalia-damage-2023-08-30/. Accessed 10 Oct. 2023.

—. "French Protests Continue over Macron's Pension Age Raise." *New York Post*, 18 Mar. 2023, nypost.com/2023/03/18/french-protests-continue-over-macrons-pension-age-raise/. Accessed 15 Oct. 2023.

—. "Putin Says Russian Forces Improving Positions along Front Line in Ukraine." *Reuters*, 15 Oct. 2023, www.reuters.com/world/europe/putin-says-russian-forces-improving-positions-along-front-line-ukraine-2023-10-15/. Accessed 16 Oct. 2023.

—. "US Scientists Repeat Fusion Ignition Breakthrough for 2nd Time." *Reuters*, 7 Aug. 2023, www.reuters.com/business/energy/us-scientists-repeat-fusion-power-breakthrough-ft-2023-08-06/. Accessed 17 Oct. 2023.

Richard, Lawrence. "China Flies More than 150 Military Planes toward Taiwan as Island Condemns Military 'Harassment.'" *Fox News*, 19 Sept. 2023, www.foxnews.com/world/china-flies-150-military-planes-toward-taiwan-island-condemns-military-harassment. Accessed 10 Oct. 2023.

Robertson, Nick. "McCarthy Hits Biden on Energy Policies: 'We're Buying It from Our Enemies.'" *The Hill*, 17 Sept. 2023, thehill.com/homenews/house/4208241-mccarthy-hits-biden-on-energy-policies/. Accessed 13 Oct. 2023.

Roth, Andrew, and Pjotr Sauer. "Russian Defector Sheds Light on Putin Paranoia and His Secret Train Network." *The Guardian*, 5 Apr. 2023, www.theguardian.com/world/2023/apr/05/russian-defector-sheds-light-on-putin-paranoia-including-secret-train. Accessed 17 Oct. 2023.

Roy, Lachmi Deb. "Harry's Hopeless Mental State; a Victim of Slow Separation as Meghan Takes Custody of Children." *Firstpost*, 15 June 2023, www.firstpost.com/entertainment/prince-harrys-hopeless-situation-is-duke-a-victim-of-slow-separation-from-meghan-12739582.html. Accessed 17 Oct. 2023.

RUGABER, CHRISTOPHER. "Wholesale Price Inflation Accelerated in August from Historically Slow Pace." *AP News*, 14 Sept. 2023, apnews.com/article/inflation-economy-federal-reserve-f0555881e11423d39d13e5790ebedbe3. Accessed 10 Oct. 2023.

Salahieh, Nouran. "At Least 99 People Were Killed in Maui's Wildfires. With Only 25% of the Burn Area Searched, Officials Worry the Death Toll Will Climb." *CNN*, 15 Aug. 2023, www.cnn.com/2023/08/15/us/hawaii-maui-wildfires-death-toll-tuesday/index.html.

SANTANA, REBECCA, and ERIC TUCKER. "US Says a Smuggler with Terrorist Ties Helped Get Migrants from Uzbekistan into the Country." *AP News*, 29 Aug. 2023, apnews.com/article/border-smuggling-terrorist-islamic-state-immigration-6d2192be5874f7f271ce28bbcc5c0473. Accessed 19 Oct. 2023.

Shaw, Adam. "Biden-Era Migrant Crisis Blowing Holes through Budgets of Liberal, Sanctuary Cities." *Fox News*, 16 Sept. 2023, www.foxnews.com/politics/biden-era-migrant-crisis-blowing-holes-through-budgets-liberal-sanctuary-cities. Accessed 20 Oct. 2023.

Space Weather. "March 2023." Spaceweather.com, 30 Mar. 2023, spaceweatherarchive.com/2023/03/. Accessed 16 Oct. 2023.

Spencer, Terry. "Hurricane Idalia Unleashes Fury on Florida after Making Landfall as a Dangerous Category 3 Storm." *AP News*, 30 Aug. 2023, apnews.com/article/florida-hurricane-idalia-2136985ceea53f5deb600c43aeea1138.

Sperry, Paul, et al. "FBI Knew All about Joe and Hunter's Business Dealings, Laptop Authenticity — and Did Nothing: Files." *New York Post*, 6 Oct. 2023, nypost.com/2023/10/06/fbi-knew-all-about-joe-and-hunters-business-dealings-laptop-authenticity-and-did-nothing-files/. Accessed 9 Oct. 2023.

TAER, JENNIE. "EXCLUSIVE: Illegal Immigration at Southern Border Hits New September Record." Dailycaller.com, 19 Oct. 2023, dailycaller.com/2023/10/19/illegal-immigration-southern-border-surges-new-september-record/. Accessed 19 Oct. 2023.

Thaler, Shannon. "Mortgage Rates near 8% as Demand Drops to 28-Year Low." *New York Post*, 4 Oct. 2023, nypost.com/2023/10/04/mortgage-rates-near-8-as-demand-drops-to-28-year-low/. Accessed 10 Oct. 2023.

The Associated Press. "Italy Cracks down on Migrants as Meloni Calls for a Naval Blockade off North Africa." *NPR*, 18 Sept. 2023, www.npr.org/2023/09/18/1200260635/italy-cracks-down-on-migrants-as-meloni-calls-for-a-naval-blockade-off-north-afr. Accessed 13 Oct. 2023.

The Moscow Times. "Russian Witches Cast Spells in Putin's Support (Video)." *The Moscow Times*, 6 Feb. 2019, www.themoscowtimes.com/2019/02/06/russian-witches-cast-spells-in-putins-support-video-a64420. Accessed 17 Oct. 2023.

The UN Refugee Agency. "Horn of Africa Food Crisis Explained." Www.unrefugees.org, 6 Apr. 2023, www.unrefugees.org/news/horn-of-africa-food-crisis-explained/#:~:text=The%20hunger%20crisis%20in%20the. Accessed 12 Oct. 2023.

Thomson-DeVeaux, Amelia. "Nikki Haley Is the First Woman of Color to Run for the Republican Nomination." *FiveThirtyEight*, 14 Feb. 2023, fivethirtyeight.com/features/nikki-haley-is-taking-on-trump/. Accessed 11 Oct. 2023.

Todd, Chuck, et al. "Poll: 68% of Voters Have Worries about Biden's Mental and Physical Health." *NBC News*, 27 June 2023, www.nbcnews.com/meet-the-press/first-read/poll-68-voters-worries-bidens-mental-physical-health-rcna91343.

*United States House Committee on Oversight and Accountability.* "Evidence of Joe Biden's Involvement in His Family's Influence Peddling Schemes." , 24 Aug. 2023, oversight.house.gov/blog/evidence-of-joe-bidens-involvement-in-his-familys-influence-peddling-schemes/.

U.S. House of Representatives. *THE BIDEN BORDER CRISIS: NEW DATA and TESTIMONY SHOW HOW the BIDEN ADMINISTRATION OPENED the SOUTHWEST BORDER and ABANDONED INTERIOR ENFORCEMENT Interim Staff Report of the Committee on the Judiciary and Subcommittee on Immigration Integrity, Security, and Enforcement.* 9 Oct. 2023, judiciary.house.gov/sites/evo-subsites/republicans-judiciary.house.gov/files/evo-media-document/2023-10-09-New-Data-and-Testimony.pdf. Accessed 20 Oct. 2023.

USA Facts. "Are Fentanyl Overdose Deaths Rising in the US?" *USAFacts*, 9 Dec. 2022, usafacts.org/articles/are-fentanyl-overdose-deaths-rising-in-the-us/. Accessed 20 Oct. 2023.

Viser, Matt, et al. "Inside Hunter Biden's Multimillion-Dollar Deals with a Chinese Energy Company." *Washington Post*, 30 Mar. 2022, www.washingtonpost.com/politics/2022/03/30/hunter-biden-china-laptop/. Accessed 12 Oct. 2023.

VOA News. "Dam Break in India's Northeast Kills at Least 31." *VOA*, 6 Oct. 2023, www.voanews.com/a/dam-break-in-india-s-northeast-kills-at-least-31/7299370.html. Accessed 11 Oct. 2023.

World Bank. "Food Security Update." *World Bank*, 22 June 2022, www.worldbank.org/en/topic/agriculture/brief/food-security-update. Accessed 12 Oct. 2023.

Yokley, Eli. "2024 GOP Primary Election Tracker | Morning Consult." *Morning Consult Pro*, 10 Oct. 2023, pro.morningconsult.com/trackers/2024-gop-primary-election-tracker. Accessed 11 Oct. 2023.

YORK, Joanna. "Inflated Rents, High Interest Rates and Lack of Supply Create European Housing Crisis." *France 24*, 3 Oct. 2023, www.france24.com/en/europe/20231003-inflated-rents-high-interest-rates-and-lack-of-supply-create-european-housing-crisis. Accessed 13 Oct. 2023.

Yu, Verna. "'We Just Want to Live in a Normal World': China's Young Protesters Speak Out, and Disappear." *The Guardian*, 8 Feb. 2023, www.theguardian.com/world/2023/feb/08/we-just-want-to-live-in-a-normal-world-chinas-young-protesters-speak-out-and-disappear. Accessed 17 Oct. 2023.

# TOPICAL INDEX

Made in the USA
Middletown, DE
29 October 2023

41518149R00106